COACHING THE GOALKEEPER

D0508393

by

Tony Waiters

WORLD of SOCCER™

Vancouver

Canadian Cataloguing in Publication Data
Waiters, Tony
Coaching the goalkeeper
(Coaching soccer series: #4)
ISBN 0-920417-07-8
1. Soccer – Goalkeeping. 2. Soccer – Coaching
1. Nichols, Martin. II. Title. III. Series.
GV943.9.9G62W34 1991 796.334'26 C91-091402-8

First Published January 6, 1992 by WORLD OF SOCCER
5880 Falcon Road, West Vancouver, British Columbia, V7W 1S3

Phone: (604) 921-8963 Fax: (604) 921-8964
Information Service: 1-800-762-2378

CREDITS

Editor: Geoff Wellens
Illustrator: Martin Nichols
Copy Processing: Susan Buckham
Layout and Design: Lionheart Graphics
Manufactured by Hemlock Printers Ltd.

First printing January 1992
Second printing February 1993
Third printing September 1993

THE COACHING SERIES:

Coaching 6, 7 and 8 year olds

Coaching 9, 10 and 11 year olds

Coaching the Team

Coaching the Goalkeeper

Coaching the Team Player

OTHER WORLD OF SOCCER PUBLICATIONS:

Teaching Offside

Soccer is Fun – A Workbook for 6, 7 and 8 Year Olds

Micro Soccer – Rules & Regulations

Coaching to Win

League Operations Manual – From 3 vs 3 to 11 vs 11

ACKNOWLEDGEMENTS

Paul Dolan
Rob Walker
Didar Sandhu
Scott Buckham

DEDICATION

To Verdi Godwin — my motivator, advisor, great friend and my only real coach.

TABLE OF CONTENTS

PUTTING IT ALL TOGETHER

SOME FINER POINTS

AN OPEN LETTER TO COACHES

In my teens I was an aspiring goalkeeper striving to find a way up. There were few coaching books, and in those that existed, there was little information about goalkeeping. There were no goalkeeper coaches and team trainers found keepers "a bit of a nuisance."

A few years later, after I had joined the professional ranks, I would go back to the clubhouse each afternoon following the regular morning practice to seek extra goalkeeper training. Most times our coach would say, "Why don't you go home and have a rest." Yeah! And dream about making that big save? Or the equipment manager would suggest, as I bugged him for some extra training kit, "Why don't you go and have a game of golf?"

He obviously did not realize I was trying to patch up the holes in my goalkeeping skills — not achieve a hole in one!

It didn't take me long to realize I was a "pain in the butt," a "nuisance," a "disruption" to their routine. Anyway, I stayed a "nuisance," and kept going back, with or without their approval.

The few that gave me that little extra (Wilf Dixon of Blackpool, Everton, Tottenham Hotspur and Arsenal, and Verdi Godwin — who didn't give a little bit, but a whole darned lot) will have my respect and appreciation forever.

Goalkeepers may cause a few problems in terms of how they fail to fit nicely into the team practice but a little attention here and there — you don't have to be a goalkeeping guru — will work wonders.

At times I claim I was a self-taught goalkeeper, but if I reflect honestly, Verdi Godwin (and Wilf Dixon) were the difference.

Coaches please consider going that extra distance — no matter how small it is — to give the goalkeepers the attention I think they deserve. They'll thank you for it — one way or another!

Tony Waiters

INTRODUCTION

Born To Play In Goal

I was born to be a soccer goalkeeper. How would it have been otherwise? I came into this world in Southport, England, 20 miles from soccer-crazy Liverpool. My mother was a sports nut. My brother Mick was three and a half years older than I…and always bigger!

So, with that background I had to play soccer. Mick had to have someone to shoot the soccer ball at and he had me tagging along.

But it wasn't exactly a case of being dragged into goal yelling and screaming. I loved it. The acrobatic and dramatic nature of the position appealed to me from Goalkeeping Day One!

Mick and I devised our own soccer games. Our favorite was Liverpool versus Newcastle. He was Liverpool. I was Newcastle United. We would play the game on Blundell's Field, the local soccer park, which was only five minutes from our home — three minutes if you ran (which we usually did!).

The rules of our game were simple. Mick was required to shoot at goal anytime, anywhere, but from no nearer the goal than the edge of the penalty box. He counted a goal every time he scored. What else? I "scored" every time I made an exceptional save. In the event of a dispute my only recourse was to appeal to the referee and arbitrator. You're right, that was Brother Mick!

These were fiercely contested games. But great fun.

Years later, when I was attending Loughborough College, training to be a Physical Education teacher, our math professor, Mr. Jones, remarking on my performances with the College team said: "The sooner Waiters realizes that goalkeeping is a mathematical science and not a series of acrobatic leaps, the sooner he will become a goalkeeper."

He was right, but only in part. The combination of positional play, of understanding angles, of calculating the percentage benefits of certain decisions, will only be successfully completed on certain occasions, by acrobatics and heroics.

The calculations and the theater of goalkeeping, plus nearly 50 years of personal goalkeeping experience of one sort or another, have produced this coaching manual.

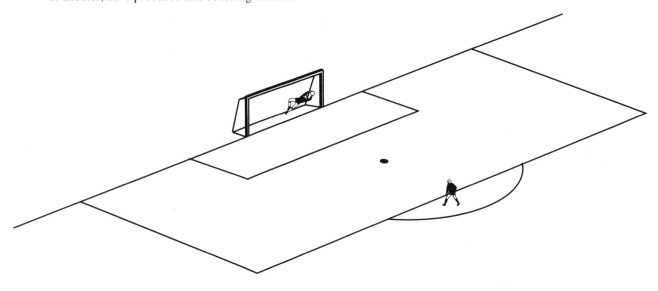

HOW TO USE THIS BOOK

This manual is not written with the expectation that the reader should go from cover to cover, nor is it in order of importance. It is your book. For you to use to your advantage.

We would recommend you look at the introductory pages so that you can ascertain the best way to approach the reading of this manual to maximize the information presented — particularly with regard to the coaching of the specific age groups with which you are involved. You will then be able to select the sections that you want for information and ideas. At the same time, we do not wish to discourage you from reading the book from start to finish and then afterwards using it as a reference resource. I believe we have compiled the book in a way that will keep your interest throughout.

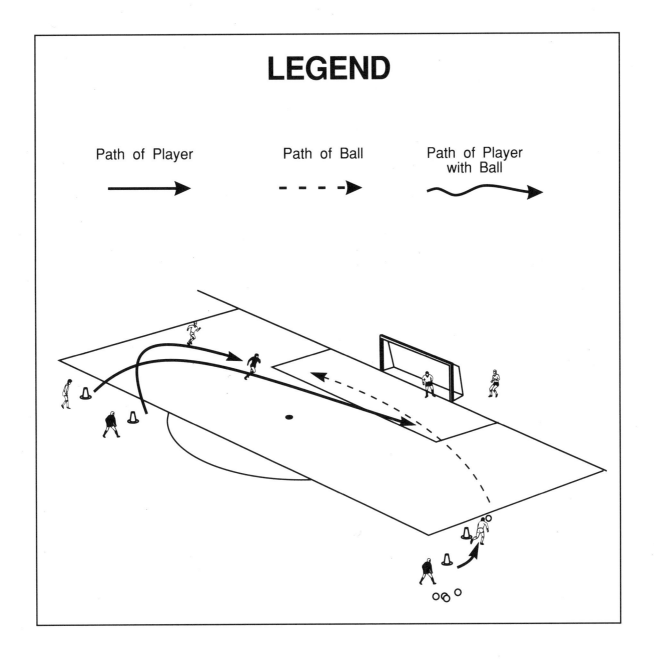

LEGEND

Path of Player

Path of Ball

Path of Player with Ball

The Goalkeeper — A Team Player

A disturbing trend has been infecting the world of soccer regarding the goalkeeper. The result has been an isolation of goalkeepers from their teammates. This trend has occurred for four main reasons:

Attitudes

The coach regards the goalkeeper as a different "animal," to be treated differently and separately from the rest of the team.

Elitism

Goalkeepers have begun to regard themselves as a breed apart and this has developed an attitude of elitism.

Specialization

The Specialist Goalkeeper Coach, and the Goalkeeper Only Schools have further fueled this development.

Equipment

The soccer supply and specialist equipment companies have capitalized on the personalization trend.

While this is understandable, it is wrong! The goalkeeper is a team player, a vital one without doubt, but no more or no less important than other players. Team play and team tactics are developed around 11 players. Not 10 players and an elitist, a freak, a goalkeeper.

A Goalkeeping Myth

One reason that coaches sometimes avoid working with goalkeepers is because of their own uncertainty. There is a fear of being wrong. Many times coaches have said to me: "What should I do with the keepers. I don't know anything about goalkeeping." Well they do! If they can coach field players, they can coach goalkeepers.

The mystique of goalkeeping is a myth. Most of goalkeeping — and goalkeeping practice — is based on common sense and the simple principles of play.

That is why we have included in this book the 12 Key Considerations (KC's). We think when you look at that section you will say to yourself, "I know that! So what's new?" In soccer, not too much! The game stands up by itself. It doesn't need gimmicks.

If the KC's do make sense then my next plea to you, the coach, is: "Get out there and give the goalkeepers some practice." The keepers will appreciate your efforts. And your contribution will be a very valuable one.

Playing the Position — Not "Performing" the Position

One factor inhibiting the development of goalkeeping in North America is the preoccupation with the athletic and acrobatic performance of the goalkeeper, rather than with effectiveness. "Looking good" doesn't necessarily mean "being good."

Good goalkeepers "play the position," they do not "perform" in the position.

The result of this preoccupation with "performing" has been an over-commitment of practice time to diving and leaping and to technique work in general, while neglecting some of the vital aspects of goalkeeping such as reading the angles, decision making, cooperation with teammates and judgment of situations and the action required. Goalkeepers must be placed in situations that test the knowledge and nerve — where, for example, a keeper may do a little more than hold a position when confronted by an opponent with the ball.

Gordon Banks, the world-class England goalkeeper of the '60s and the '70s, is probably best remembered for his magnificent one-handed flying save off a goalbound header from the legendary Pele in the 1970 World Cup in Mexico. The reality is, Gordon Banks would never have been around Mexico to make that fabulous save if his basic goalkeeping and understanding of goalkeeping had not been absolutely sound.

Amongst the professionals, Gordon Banks was known and respected for being an unspectacular goalkeeper who did the simple things often and well. It helped make him the best in the world!

Goalkeeper Now a Footballer

As the tactical role of the goalkeepers change, we see them moving outside of the penalty area more frequently than in the past. This may be to clear a dangerous situation, to take a free kick, to advance with the ball when the opposition has dropped back. As well, recent rule changes ask more of a goalkeeper's foot skills than they ever did in the past and coaches and goalkeepers should welcome this opportunity for the keeper to become more of an all-round player — a team player!

Therefore, kicking, passing and ball control practices are essential for a keeper. The goalkeeper can now become a legitimate part of practices that in previous years had been presented for the benefit of field players.

NAIVE IN CONCEPT?

As I was finishing my English 1st Division playing career at Blackpool Football Club, I was invited to be a guest instructor at the Blackpool Easter School. This was a Football Association Certification course conducted primarily for teachers during their Easter vacation.

The director of the school was an old friend of mine, Arthur Etchells, a staff coach of the English Football Association. Arthur was a lecturer in Physical Education and had been a top rugby player before turning to the teaching and coaching of soccer. Years earlier, Arthur had put me on the road to my coaching career when I took my Preliminary "badge." He was the course conductor.

On the occasion of the Easter School, I "guested" for a two-hour afternoon session by presenting the "Key Considerations in the Coaching of Goalkeepers." Later that day, in a discussion amongst the school staff coaches, (which I only heard about later), one described my presentation as "naive in concept" — whatever that may have meant! My lecture that afternoon was based on 25 years of goalkeeping experience, the last eight of those years in the English 1st Division and four of those eight spent with the England World Cup Team. It was a summary of my life involvement with goalkeeping.

A year after the Blackpool School, Charles Hughes, at the time assistant director of coaching for the Football Association, asked me, at the eleventh hour, to present another "Coaching of Goalkeepers" demonstration to a gathering of managers and head coaches of English League clubs. This was at Lilleshall, now the Football Association National Training Center. My session through necessity and lack of preparation time, was almost identical to the one in Blackpool.

The outcome of the session this time was that I was offered a coaching position at the mighty Liverpool Football Club. Bill Shankly, their legendary managing coach, said the clinching factor was that the presentation "was simple and understandable."

Writing a soccer manual is not so simple, but I hope to make it clear to you the reader — the coach — that the teaching of goalkeeping, and the information presented to goalkeepers, does not have to be complicated; that the goalkeeping position is not complex, and that what I am suggesting to you is not "naive in concept!"

AGE CONSIDERATIONS

AGES 6-11

No permanent player "positions." 11-a-side not suitable for this age group. Experience given to all players in most facets of the game — including goalkeeping.

Two main goalkeeper teaching considerations:

- Catching ball in front of the body with palms to the ball.
- Diving for shots and the tumbling involved.

AGES 12-15

Decisions by players and coaches now needed regarding "their positions."

Care and discretion required in selection of "permanent" positions (future physique and development of abilities?).

Players must not be "locked" into the goalkeeping position.

Practice and coaching for goalkeepers in: Shot Stopping; Crosses; Through Balls — with emphasis on technique.

Kicking and Throwing (very important).

Furthering the understanding of the goalkeeper's role.

AGES 16+

"Putting it all together."

Physique almost established — therefore, specialization in "positions."

Creates emphasis on the tactical role of the goalkeeper.

"Playing the Position" — understanding of the requirements.

Much practice involving decision making — without ignoring basic techniques of Shot Stopping, Staying on Feet, Narrowing Angles, Catching Crosses, Kicking and Throwing.

AGES 25+

The Glory Years — from 25 - 35.

Positional play. Temperament. Decision making.

Maturity and experience.

Maintaining position and "playing the percentages."

The nerve and ability to do the job right.

COACHING 6 - 11 YEAR OLDS

All Players/All Goalkeepers

We have already indicated that players in this age group should not have taken up any of the permanent positions of the adult game. Sweepers, strikers, stoppers, midfielders, wingers, permanent goalkeepers are for the sophisticated and tactical game of soccer chess that comes when, and only when, coaches have given up on players so far as all-round skill development is concerned, and have begun to "maximize" the team strengths and "minimize" the individual weaknesses.

"He could never score a goal in a million years!" (Interpretation — "Keep that player as far from the goal as possible!") "She's absolutely hopeless in the air." (Interpretation — "Keep the player out of the center of the defense and the attack." Looks like our "headless" player will end up in a flank position.)

None of our 6 - 11 year olds are "hopeless." Nor can any of them be a great goalkeeper yet! Therefore, we must not deny any young player the opportunity to develop all-round skills.

So, our strong recommendation is that all players have an opportunity to develop goalkeeping skills — particularly from ages 6 - 9. And let them all have fun while they are doing it.

What Skills to Concentrate on?

Later in the book we will make reference to the practices which we would particularly recommend as most suitable to this age group.

The first skill that young players find difficult is catching the ball soccer goalkeeper fashion. In soccer the keeper should always present both palms of the hand outwards to the incoming ball (see Key Considerations — The Hands). This catching technique is unique to soccer goalkeeping. This is the place to start, and as you will see with "Catch and Hug" (Page 59) this can give practice in the Throw In technique as well (most kids experience difficulty with Throw Ins as well as catching the ball goalkeeper fashion).

The second most-difficult area is the necessity at times, for all goalkeepers to have to dive to save the ball. Again a soccer goalkeeper needs a specific diving technique, unlike any other sport or gymnastic movement. Initially most players will be reluctant to dive, so we need a graduated progression. In the end everything will turn out fine because we know kids love to tumble and fall.

Finally, the aspect of throwing a soccer ball is not easy for children with small hands and a lack of strength, especially if the wrong type and size of soccer ball is used (the Micro Soccer Ball or a size 3 or size 4 ball are recommended). Never use the size 5 ball at this age.

So kicking and throwing and catching and diving are important goalkeeping skills to be developed at this age. What else should we cover? Not much! In the early years of soccer most children see the goalkeeper role as one of "on the goal line stopping the shots." And they are right!

Shot stopping is the basis of good goalkeeping. So why should we be concerning ourselves at this age with "narrowing the angle," "coming off the line" to field a crossed ball or running out to "dive at the feet" of an incoming forward.

Let's face it! Kids are not yet ready for that level of goalkeeping. And if put in those circumstances, they would almost certainly get themselves and others injured.

Goalkeeping Organization

As all young players should be involved as goalkeepers and as field players, and as most of the goalkeeping practice should surround catching, throwing, kicking and shot stopping, use of markers for goals with everyone participating will quickly get your players off and running…or should it be diving?

Goalkeeping activities fit very neatly into the warm-up phase of practice (8 - 10 minutes). A catch and throw activity for instance, will work well before moving into other fun games and practices (see *Coaching 6, 7 & 8 Year Olds* and *Coaching 9, 10 & 11 Year Olds*).

Recommendations to Coaches of 6 - 11 Year Olds

Read the section on the Key Considerations and then refer to the following recommended practices:

- Pendulum Roll (Page 40)

- Squat Thrust (Page 41)

- Catch and Hug (Page 59)

- Two Goal Practice (Page 58)

- Three-Shot Stop (Page 43)

- Wheeling and Dealing (Page 46)

- Criss-Cross (Page 48)

- Submarining (9, 10 & 11's only — Page 50)

- No Sleeper Keeper (9, 10 & 11's only — Page 82)

- GK Ball (Page 80)

COACHING 12 - 15 YEAR OLDS

It is at this age that teams begin to move into serious competitive 11-a-side play, and yet most players should not have established a "permanent" position within the team. For field players flexibility of position is much easier to accomplish than that of a goalkeeper. Once the GK jersey and gloves have been donned, chances are that player is permanently labeled.

In many cases "goalkeeper" is the position the player wishes to play. Persuading the would-be "goalkeeper" that it may not necessarily be in their best interests to "lock" themselves into that position could be difficult — particularly if the keeper is a "good one."

Sometimes the coach is the "guilty party" in encouraging a certain player to be the keeper, because that player is the best equipped — the most competent person for the position — and it greatly assists the overall team performance. The fact is that this age is a transitional one regarding the establishment of positions, and some sensitivity and philosophical reflection is necessary regarding the goalkeeping role.

In the early stages (12 and 13 years), the coach should move away from giving everyone the opportunity of goalkeeping training (as we recommended in the years between 6 and 11), but should still encourage a pool of goalkeepers (say of 4 - 6). Perhaps the coach can employ some kind of rotation system on game day (2 or 3 sharing the goalkeeping duties one week, 2 or 3 the next). Even though it may present some equipment and uniform problems it is worth considering. More final decisions on "permanent" positions will be made in the next age phase (16+).

At this age, the basics of goalkeeping are still at the core of the coaching and training program — shot stopping, diving and catching techniques, kicking and throwing development. However, a sizeable percentage of practice time now needs to be devoted to "narrowing the angle," "dealing with through balls," "cross ball situations" and simple "tactical considerations."

All of the practices included in this manual give recommendations regarding the suitability of each practice to each age group.

It is strongly recommended that the segment concerned with the 12 KC's is studied in its entirety and then the practices that are particularly suited to "team practice" situations are considered first and foremost.

These are as follows:

- Gone Fishing (Page 60)
- Wheeling and Dealing (Page 46)
- Near and Far (Page 72)
- Through Balls (Page 62)
- Side Kicks (Page 66)
- No Sleeper Keeper (Page 82)
- Criss-Cross (Page 48)

- Diving Headers (Page 64)
- GK's Chip 'n Dale (Page 76)
- Let's Dance (Page 52)
- GK Ball (Page 80)
- Mixed Bag (Page 78)
- Big Shot (Page 86)
- Super 8's (Page 84)

The coach should also consider additional sessions exclusively for the would-be goalkeepers. This can be at the beginning or the end of the team practice (or even during the practice with the help of an assistant coach). Also there is the possibility of the goalkeepers finding some additional development opportunities (clinics, keeper schools, on-going goalkeeping programs, etc.).

In addition to the Team GK Practices the following should be included in a goalkeeping program outside the normal team practice:

- Pendulum Roll (Page 40)
- Salmon Leap (Page 44)
- Two Goal Practice (Page 58)
- Shadow Goalkeeping (Page 54)
- Six-Shot Stop (Page 42)
- Submarining (Page 50)

If it is possible to conduct one or two of the above drills for 10 minutes at the conclusion of the team practices just for the "goalkeepers," that would be great. It may need some organization and sacrifice to make it possible, but I know the rewards will be worth the effort.

GOOD GOALKEEPERS ARE LIKE GOOD WINES

Good goalkeepers are like good wines — they get better with age. But then only for so long!

The age considerations presented above, are just general guidelines. One 16 year old may be more like the average 19 year old, another more like a 13 year old.

We have to be careful about "labeling" young players once and for all. The best young (13 year old) goalkeeper I ever saw failed to make the top flight of the game because he never grew. At 20 years of age he was no taller than he was at 13. In the end, it was not technique or know-how, he was just too short.

Dino Zoff, Peter Shilton and Pat Jennings all played in World Cup Finals as goalkeepers at 40 years of age. So what's the hurry?

COACHING 16+ GOALKEEPERS

By this time the reality of soccer has usually struck home, both to players and to coaches. The best position, both for a player's strengths and weaknesses, is becoming much more apparent (although nothing should be "cast in concrete"). By this time, our goalkeepers have usually made a commitment to the position.

While the basics of goalkeeping — the techniques of shot stopping, diving at the feet, catching and punching crosses, kicking and throwing techniques — are still needed, this is the time when decision-making practices are critically important if the goalkeeper is to become a true Team Goalkeeper.

The relevant games and drills of the practice session have to be applied (see below) to enable a goalkeeper to become an effective member of the team unit.

There is no such thing as the "perfect goalkeeper" so there will be some basic techniques that still need developing or correcting. If, for instance, there is a problem in "Side Diving" then a BACK-TO-BASICS (BTB) practice routine such as the Six-Shot Stop (Page 42) should be factored into the program.

In addition, a "maintenance" program is required for all the basic facets of goalkeeping in order to maintain "touch" and "sharpness." Nevertheless, the team decision-making situations should assume the greatest importance. Recommended practices are:

- GK's Chip 'n Dale (Page 76)
- Crossroads (Page 74)
- Near and Far (Page 72)
- Mixed Bag (Page 78)
- Big Shot (Page 86)
- Super 8's (Page 84)

GOAL SIZES IN PRACTICE

From age 16 upwards, when practicing with improvised goals (cones/corner flags), it is a good idea to make sure the goal is standard size. Using a 6- or 7-yard-wide goal could establish bad habits and a false sense of security.

In fact, I would recommend going the other way by having goals wider than 8 yards (9 yards max.) to produce that extra spring and effort.

In a game, if there is any doubt about whether the ball is going just wide, or just inside the post, it is no fun making embarrassed explanations later. Better to be on the safe side even at the cost of a corner-kick.

THE KEY CONSIDERATIONS

INTRODUCTION TO THE KC's

There are many factors in the make up and the development process of the goalkeeper. So where do you start?

From my experience everything comes back to 12 Key Considerations — what we have termed in this book, The KC's of Goalkeeping. These are, in the main, very simple and based on common sense. But most of all they are based on the hard experience of many professional goalkeepers, myself included.

Once these 12 Key Considerations are understood, any coach can give first-class and appropriate advice to any goalkeeper, young or mature, experienced or novice.

We have presented these "Key Considerations" in a way that should stick in the mind. We have used acronyms and goalkeeping "buzz words" to help the understanding of the development process — both for you and for your goalkeepers.

Whether you use the phrases or not, is unimportant — your call — but understanding the Key Considerations is very important. They form the basis to your success in assisting the development of your goalkeepers.

USE THIS SECTION AS A REFERENCE SEGMENT

This segment of the book concerning the "Key Considerations" has been placed near the beginning deliberately. Much of what comes after will refer back to these KC's.

Don't think you have to go through this chapter page by page, word by word. If it holds your attention first time through — fine! If not, move on. There will be plenty of time and encouragement to return.

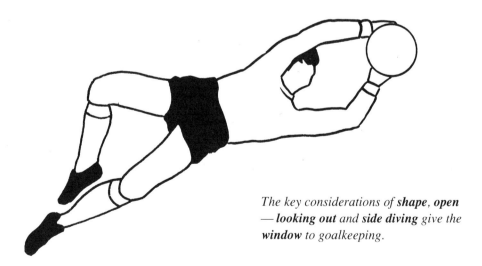

*The key considerations of **shape**, **open** — **looking out** and **side diving** give the **window** to goalkeeping.*

THE 12 KEY CONSIDERATIONS

A Dozen Ways To Simplify Goalkeeping

The Hands — the "King" Consideration.

Shape — goalkeeping posture; Concaving; The Gorilla.

Alert and Alive — ready and relaxed — and Dancing!

Open — Looking Out — the window to the world.

Absorption — the Octopus; "Have you hugged your ball today?"

AMOB III — as Much of the Body Behind the Ball as possible.

"Stay on your Feet" — ALAP (as long as possible).

"Don't Fall Backwards!"

Set! . . . and Go!

Side Diving — to the side and on the side.

"React" — do not Anticipate!

Recovery — AQAP (as quickly as possible).

THE HANDS

The King Consideration

The feature that distinguishes the goalkeeper from the rest of the team is the ability of the goalkeeper to use the hands within the defending penalty area. No other player is legally allowed to use the hands (other than at a throw-in).

Not only does this rule allow the goalkeeper a distinct advantage, it also becomes the biggest consideration in how the goalkeeper goes about the task of defending the goal.

The Hands are The Leaders

Both palms of the hands must always be turned outwards to the ball. Anatomically this means the body position will have to be adjusted to ensure that both palms and not just one can be in position to do just that. The object is to present the maximum amount of palm and fingers to the ball.

High "W" hand position.
The "W" is formed by the thumbs
and index fingers.

"High piano" hand position

"Welcome" position

"Jellyfish" hand position.

Back view of the "W" hand position

The King Consideration of both hands/palms being presented to the ball will only change in occasional circumstances. The two main ones being:

When a goalkeeper is at full stretch and is only able to get full extension of the body by angling the shoulders to make the one-handed save.

When a goalkeeper elects to punch the ball with one or two fists when moving into heavy traffic.

Hands — Arms — Shoulders

In soccer, for field players, the "hand ball" rule does not just apply to the hands but to the arms as well.

In a similar way the goalkeeper must regard the arms and hands as the same thing. If the arms are not right the hands cannot do their job.

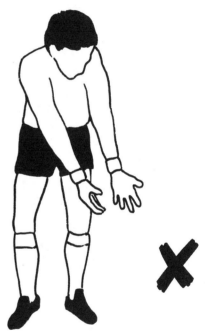

As we see in the illustration, if an arm is pulled across the body the palm of that hand cannot do the job of facing the ball. So the hands must lead but the rest of the body must follow the lead to allow the required hand position to take place.

The hands and arms bring us to the shoulders, and all goalkeepers (and their coaches) should be aware of the importance of shoulder position. If the shoulders are square to the ball (e.g. facing the ball) the goalkeeper's body position will not be far wrong.

As well, the squareness of the shoulders allows the keeper to form a "window" — so important to successful performance. If the "window" is closed, there is a good chance of imminent goalkeeping disaster.

Both palms must face the ball — only possible when the body is "arranged" to assist the hand position.

Finally, with the hands leading — in front of the body, yet not at full stretch (with the crooked elbow giving a strongly absorbing effect) a margin for error is built in as we will see when studying the KC's of Absorption and Side Diving.

SHAPE

The posture of the true goalkeeper would alienate any drill sergeant anywhere in the world. The best looking goalkeepers are always round shouldered, and look more like a gorilla than a U.S. marine. This "concaving" of the body assists in every facet of the actions of the goalkeeper.

Even when saving the ball on the ground or in the air, the "concaving" principle and body shape are critically important.

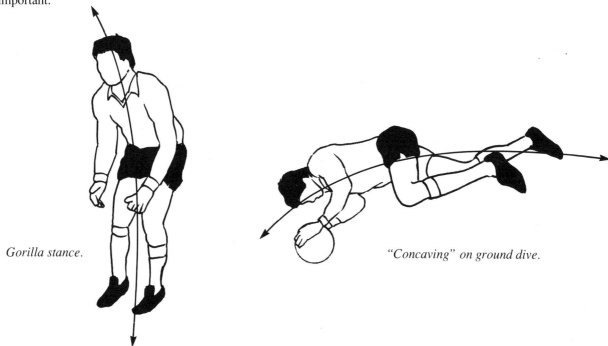

Gorilla stance.

"Concaving" on ground dive.

Only when things are a little "out of control" and the goalkeeper is forced into a full stretch save will the "concaving" posture be surrendered. While this may be the one of the most exciting moments of goalkeeping, it also is the time when all else has failed — a time for desperate last-ditch action. These "desperate actions" need to be practiced to put "the icing on the cake," but good goalkeepers, by their positioning and "reading" of the situations will keep these desperate moments of glory to a minimum. Flying saves are great, but if they are being made continually, chances are, the keeper does not understand positional play. Good goalkeepers don't play for 50/50 situations.

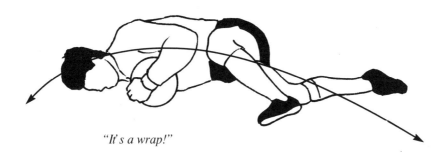

"It's a wrap!"

Ideally, in most goalkeeping acts, the final move should be one where the body is comfortably wrapping itself around the ball.

ALERT, ALIVE AND READY

The goalkeeper is a dancer — forever moving in a controlled, flowing, and rhythmic way. There is not a time, nor a place on the soccer field, where the keeper should be standing still — other than in one situation! "At penalty kicks" you say? Wrong! Even at penalty kicks, although the keeper cannot move the feet until the kick is taken, the rest of the body, including the hands and arms, can move.

No! The only time the goalkeeper is still is to "set" a split second before a shot. We will deal with that consideration when we look at the "Set" KC later.

Alert! Alive! — and Dancing!

At all other times, the goalkeeper should be moving backwards, forwards and sideways, adjusting to the movement of the ball. Even at stoppages in the game, such as injuries and substitutions, the keeper should be dancing, concentrating, staying on the toes, remaining alert and alive…and always "ready!"

As the play moves down the field the keeper should move out of goal, even as far as the edge of the penalty area (sometimes beyond). As play comes back, the keeper adjusts backwards and as the play is switched from one side of the field to the other, the goalkeeper's position is adjusted accordingly.

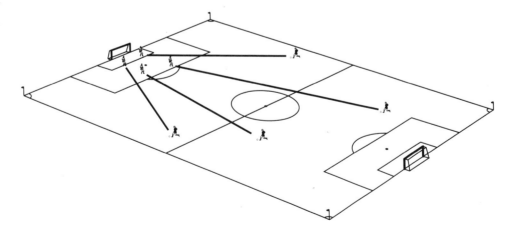

Good goalkeepers know within an inch just where they are in the penalty area. There should be no need to look back at the goalposts. They don't move anyway! Field markings, such as the "D" on the edge of the penalty box, the penalty area markings themselves, the penalty spot, the goalposts and corner flags at the other end of the field, can be used to assist in the calculation of exactly where a goalkeeper is at any moment in time.

OPEN — LOOKING OUT

The Key Considerations do not work in isolation. They all depend on each other and overlap. The "Open—Looking Out" combination is all part of "Shape," "the Hands," and other KC's.

The "window" of goalkeeping is created by body and arms.

The "Open — Looking Out" consideration advises that the goalkeeper's body should always be "open" to the ball (and to the field of play). The goalkeeper must be "looking out" by adjusting body and arms to get a clear "shoulders-to-the-ball" view of the action.

The goalkeeper must then keep the "GK window" open.

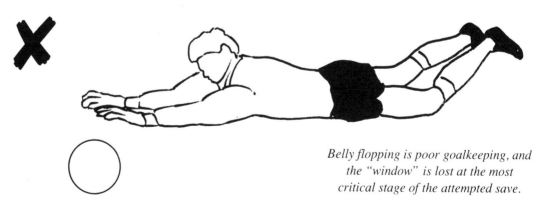

Belly flopping is poor goalkeeping, and the "window" is lost at the most critical stage of the attempted save.

Turning your back on people is considered impolite.

Turning your back on the ball isn't impolite — it's bad goalkeeping.

ABSORPTION

Goalkeepers don't catch the ball, they "receive" it. It is similar to a field player controlling the ball where the withdrawing movement of the leg, thigh or chest takes the pace off the ball. Having received the ball, the keeper normally "hides" it away from the opposition.

The soaring goalkeeper still needs the "shock absorbers" provided by "crooked" elbows.

Obviously, the hands, as already stated, give the goalkeeper a distinct advantage, and this must be capitalized upon. The act of catching is to "receive" the ball by reaching out to "welcome" the ball.

The goalkeeper "shape" may be that of a gorilla, but the capturing of the ball is more like the action of an octopus — with the tentacles reaching out and drawing in the victim. But there the analogy ends, because the ball should be treated like a son or daughter — to be handled firmly yet gently, to be welcomed and hugged not pushed away. So we might well ask our goalkeepers: "Have you hugged your ball today?"

The hands and arms act, wherever possible, like shock absorbers — to take the sting and pace out of the ball. In order to do this the hands/arms must be forward of the body, with crooked elbows giving that built-in absorption.

"Receiving" the ball in front of the body.

To gain the "shock absorber" benefits, the ball should be received whenever possible without the arms at full stretch. The "crooked elbow" posture is the ideal for receiving and absorbing the ball. It also allows a margin for error in the case of a misjudgment, where it may be necessary to stretch a few inches more than was first assessed. Also, as will be further explained in the Side Diving KC, it allows for the cushioning and trapping of the ball as the body comes down to earth at the completion of a diving save.

BODY BEHIND THE BALL

The AMOB III consideration of getting **As Much of the Body Behind the Ball** as possible is obvious, common-sense, simple — but essential!

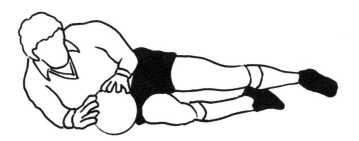

It could be that the merest touch of the finger tips is as much of the body as the keeper can get behind the ball on a particular save. Other times it could be the hands, arms plus a further part of the body. At Goalkeeping Clinics, I sometimes tease young goalkeepers by claiming that I used to grow my finger nails long just to give me a bit more "body" to make the emergency save.

Ideally, in getting "as much of the body behind the ball as possible," it is preferable to have "double insurance" — where two parts of the body are behind the ball, in case the first part fails. The hands will almost always be the first part of the body behind the ball, but the added insurance of the head or chest, stomach or legs will pay dividends — and avoid embarrassment.

It goes further than that. It is better to get muscle and soft tissue as the "back-up" rather than bony surfaces. For example, the shins give poor double cover, as do the knees, because the ball bounces off these surfaces. On the other hand, the stomach is excellent — giving a large (not too large, I hope) muscled area that, by comparison to bone, is softer and more absorbent.

I have joked (perhaps semi-joked) with aspiring goalkeepers that it is better to have the face as back-up rather than the upper chest for shoulder high shots. "Rather a bloody nose than a goal." Not the coaching point you would make to a would-be 12 year old goalkeeper — but to a prospective Olympian or Professional — yes!

The hands will always be the key factor in the success of the goalkeeper — the "King" Consideration. Nothing is certain. Cover is the essence of good defending in soccer. AMOB III — as much of the body behind the ball as possible — is the "cover insurance" of goalkeeping and essential for consistent success.

"Have you hugged your ball today?"

"STAY ON YOUR FEET"

One of our Key Considerations — "Shape" — likens the posture of a goalkeeper to that of a gorilla. Faced one-on-one by a gorilla, I'd rather take my chances with the gorilla lying on the ground, than against a gorilla standing up facing me.

Good goalkeepers are not forever flying around the goal area like Peter Pan. Nor are good goalkeepers noted for "lying down on the job." The ability to make the flying save and the quick-reaction ground save can move the good goalkeeper into the "outstanding" category, but most of the goalkeeper's work will be done "on the feet."

"Beat me if you can!"

The KC says "Stay on your feet as long as possible…" Inevitably there will come a time when the keeper will have to spread to dive at the feet of a incoming forward or react with a sideways diving leap for the shot that cannot be properly gathered otherwise. This is the calculation. As we will explain in more detail later, the goalkeeper should "react" rather than "anticipate." "Beat me if you can!" should be the attitude and posture of the goalkeeper as opponents shape up to score a goal.

Great goal scorers have the composure and ability when in front of the goal to wait until the last split second before executing their shot. They know their task may be simplified by a goalkeeper "flopping" like a beached seal. Better to be like the awesome gorilla by "staying on the feet as long as possible," and so putting the onus and the responsibility on the shooter.

"DON'T FALL BACKWARDS"

If it makes sense to stay on your feet as long as possible, it makes sense not to fall backwards when reacting to a shot. The "concaving" gorilla shape automatically brings the goalkeeper onto the toes.

Any recoiling movement backwards — either arching the body or a "sitting" posture — puts the balance of the body back on the heels. From the "on-the-toes" position the reactive saving area is vastly greater than from an "on-the-heels" position.

*On-the-toes and in the gorilla position
gives the potential of a much larger
defending area.*

Even if the "falling back" goalkeeper gets lucky and the ball hits the body, unless it "sticks" (unlikely with this posture), the keeper will be in a poor position on the ground to "recover" to face the next part of the action. That is one — but only one — reason for the importance of diving to and on the side.

SET — AND GO!

As I pointed out earlier, I sometimes ask the question of goalkeepers and coaches, "When is the only time a goalkeeper does not move?" The regular response is: "At a penalty kick." Wrong.

The only time a goalkeeper is completely still, and then only momentarily, is just before a shot is taken. Once the positions have been calculated, moved to, and the final adjustments made, then immediately before the shot is taken the body is "SET," gorilla shape, to enable the goalkeeper to react — upwards, sideways, even forwards (hopefully not backwards) — to the shot. Of course, the shot may not be taken and so the situation changes. In those circumstances, the adjustments, positional considerations, and the decision making continues, until the requirement to "set" comes once again.

It is essential that in the "Set" position not only is the gorilla shape adopted, but the body weight is evenly distributed on both feet.

Cannot dive sideways from this stance.

If the body is moving forward at the time of the shot it is almost impossible to dive sideways.

If the body weight is transferred to one side — to one foot — it's almost impossible to dive to the other side.

The attitude and posture should be — I am "**SET**," and for this moment in time I'm "staying-on-my-feet." Now score if you can! Which brings us nicely to the next KC…

SIDE DIVING

When everything else has been calculated and executed, the dive can be "the icing on the cake" — the spectacular, yet every so often, essential part of good goalkeeping.

Diving on-the-side and to-the-side are two critically vital factors in goalkeeping.

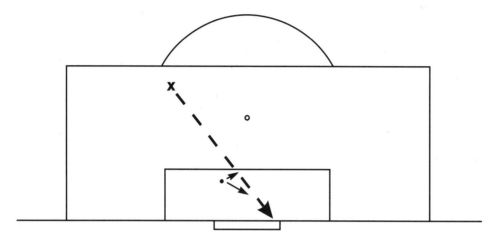

Because goalkeepers should attack the ball with their hands and arms in front of their body, the side diving is in fact, a slightly forward dive. The backwards diving goalkeeper in the above diagram has bought more time in an attempt to make the save, but has lost distance — and maybe a goal.

Attacking the ball with the side dive will be based on time, the reactions of a goalkeeper, and will be linked in with physique. a smaller, quicker goalkeeper will look to take the quickest, shortest route to the ball. The bigger keeper may look for a fraction more time because of slower reactions. The advantage is of size and reach but the big keeper must not loose too much "size" by flopping backwards.

With so many advantages to the side diving position, it is not worth considering any other way.

*Landing position stablized by bringing
in the upper knee and leaving the lower
leg trailing.*

The landing position, particularly when the upper knee is brought across, and with the lower leg trailing (see illustration on the previous page) is the most comfortable and the least "bone-shaking."

The Open — Looking Out position is maintained and the "window" to the ball is kept open.

Whether the ball is secured or not, the side diving landing position, as will be explained later, affords the best body position to quickly recover to the feet.

The side diving position allows the hands and arms to be in front of the body, and allows the hands and arms to adjust after catching the ball to the impact with the ground. The arms and hand position are adjusted to help hold the ball and to cushion the fall.

The Side Position is the best for making a recovery save after a partial save, enabling a partial recovery before launching again.

Belly Flopping is painful in the swimming pool, and definitely not recommended on the soccer field. Also victory rolls and rolling on the back are not recommended for those who want to become "good goalkeepers."

For additional information on **side diving**, see page 98.

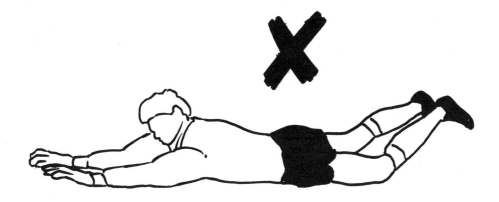

REACT — DO NOT ANTICIPATE!

"Reading the game" is an oft-used expression in soccer. It describes situations where good players use their experience to improve their decision making in terms of movement and positional play.

Anticipating where a shot is going is not recommended for young goalkeepers. "Second guessing" the shooter may be an embarrassing and incorrect exercise.

"I thought he was going to put it to my right."

"He mishit the shot! He meant to put it the other side." But he didn't!

So, good goalkeepers will "play the percentages" and should not sacrifice good positions by anticipating the striker.

Many times a shot hits a well-positioned goalkeeper. "Lucky keeper!" is the shout. Only when it has happened on a regular basis will the observers begin to realize that it is not just luck. It's good goalkeeping.

Of course, reactions have to be sharpened so that the keeper can "play the percentages" and still make that last-ditch save by a quick reaction to the circumstances that unfold. But goalkeepers cannot make things happen. The opposition has the ball. Keepers can only respond — react — to the situations they face.

RECOVERY

It's obvious that if the goalkeeper does not have the ball secured in the hands, the last place a goalkeeper should be is lying on the ground.

Therefore, "RECOVERY" back to the feet is a Key Consideration in the art and science of goalkeeping.

Down — but not out!

"Victory rolls" after a one-handed save are all very well — providing the ball has gone out of play for a corner-kick. If the ball is still in play as a result of a partial save, a deflection onto the post or bar, then the "victory roll" is not appropriate. The keeper had better get back to his or her feet P.D.Q.

"Recovery" is all tied in to the Side Diving and the Open considerations, but does need practice. It is a physical (almost a gymnastic) movement. The Six-Shot Stop practice (Page 42) is a perfect example of a GK drill that helps develop the physical requirements of the "Recovery" consideration.

THE PRACTICES

All the practices that follow have been presented in a similar way. The practices are each set out on two pages.

On the left hand side page is the name of the picture and a brief description (**OBJECTIVES**). This is followed by an illustration and a written description of the practice (**ORGANIZATION**), and notes about the most important teaching and learning factors that will occur (**COACHING POINTS**).

At the bottom of each left hand page is a panel describing the abilities that are developed by the practice (**ABILITIES DEVELOPED**) and the **KEY CONSIDERATIONS (KC's EMPHASIZED)** that are highlighted and developed by the practice.

On the right hand side page is **ADDITIONAL INFORMATION**. This page will give a further insight into how the practice can be progressed, simplified or modified for younger players and other considerations.

Finally, there is a panel outlining the age considerations, the suitability of the particular practice to the age groups, and some brief comments about the applicability of the practice to that age (**AGE, SUITABILITY, COMMENTS**).

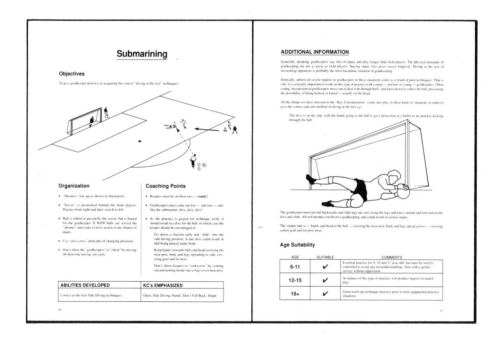

The total practice section is split into three segments:

SPECIFIC SKILLS — practices or drills that highlight one particular skill (e.g. side diving).

COMBINED SKILLS — practices that are relatively uncomplicated but require decisions by the keeper as to the action and the skills to be employed.

GAME DECISION SITUATIONS — practices that "bring it together" with decision making, communication and the goalkeeping performance affected by tactical considerations for the team play.

PRACTICES EMPHASIZING SPECIFIC SKILLS

Pendulum Roll

Objectives

To give practice in the correct landing techniques involved in side diving.

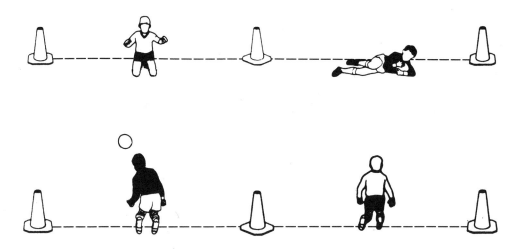

Organization

- Set out as many "goals" as there are "goalkeepers."

- Two goalkeepers per area, one with a ball, both kneel facing one another four yards apart.

- Important that the players kneel in an upright position and do not sit back on their heels.

- Balls must be rolled to the side of each keeper — not straight — but not so far to the side that the receiver cannot roll over and collect the ball.

- After receiving the ball the keeper should "roll" back to the kneeling position.

Coaching Points

- Hands and arms should reach forward to catch ball in front of body.

- Arms should not be at full stretch — but "crooked."

- Upper knee should be drawn in comfortably across the body as the ball is received.

- Lower leg should remain loosely trailing.

- Head and upper shoulder should be drawn over and above the height of the ball.

- "W" hand position is employed but with ball "trapped" by the upper hand on top of the ball and lower hand behind the ball.

ABILITIES DEVELOPED	KC's EMPHASIZED
Introduction to the best way of diving for the ball.	Side Diving, Open, Recovery, Absorption, Hands, Shape, AMOB III.

ADDITIONAL INFORMATION

The "W" hand position, but this time with the ball trapped on the ground by the positioning of the hands at the top and back of the ball, is an important technique to develop in relation to diving and retaining the ball after the impact on landing.

As players become comfortable with the **Pendulum Roll**, the practice can be progressed to the **Squat Thrust** where a squat position is adopted to receive the throw. Because of the greater leaping potential of the **Squat Thrust** the ball can be thrown further to the side of the diving player than from the kneeling position.

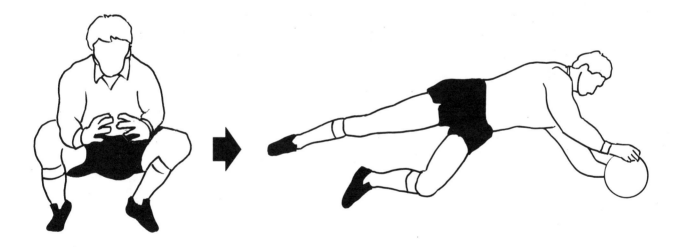

Age Suitability

AGE	SUITABLE	COMMENTS
6-11	✔	Essential activity, which all of the team can do as a warm-up activity.
12-15	✔	Essential Back-to-Basics (BTB) exercise to ensure the maintenance of good side diving techniques.
16+	✔	Good basic work which can be incorporated in a warm-up routine.

Six-Shot Stop

Objectives

To practice the diving and recovery techniques involved in shots on goal.

Organization

- Coach stands approximately 5-6 yards from the goal.

- Coach has one ball in hand and 2 or 3 others close by.

- The coach simulates shots at goal by rolling to the side; lobbing over the head; throwing ball downwards to replicate a downwards header; but always giving the keeper a chance to save.

- If the keeper misses the ball, or pushes the shot away or over the bar, coach picks up another ball while keeper is recovering back to feet.

- When keeper catches the ball — this is most important — keeper must first throw the ball back to the server before doing anything else, and use momentum of the throw to aid the recovery back to the Alert and Alive position.

Coaching Points

- Must dive on side.

- Must keep lower leg trailing and bring upper knee in (and not upwards) across body.

- Throw ball back to server and "pump" upper knee back straight to aid recovery. (Although this practice might appear artificial, particularly the condition of asking for the ball to be thrown back to the coach before starting the full recovery off the ground, it is an excellent method for developing the side diving and recovery requirements.)

ABILITIES DEVELOPED	KC's EMPHASIZED
Reactions, Handling, Power Diving.	Side Diving, Open, Recovery, Absorption, Hands.

ADDITIONAL INFORMATION

Throwing the ball back from the side diving position, while pumping back up with the upper knee, brings the correct Recovery position, and forces the Side Diving and Open KC's to be adopted.

This "artificial" practice requires the keeper to throw the ball back to the server, something that would never be done in a game. But the effect of the "condition" is to compel the goalkeeper to adopt an "open" side-diving position when making the save — otherwise it would be impossible to return the ball.

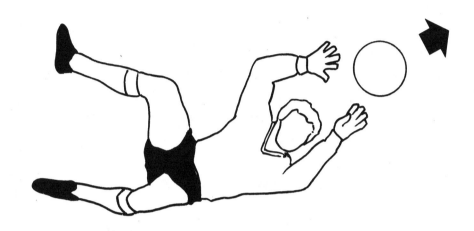

If the goalkeeper swings both knees round, dives backwards, belly flops, or rolls on the back, it is impossible to "recover" quickly. The exercise therefore, establishes good diving techniques and good basic habits.

Six shots is considered the maximum number. After six repetitions fatigue may set in, and the keeper may start "flapping and flopping." This type of sloppy play must be discouraged at all times. Coaches must remember, this is not an endurance or fitness exercise. It is a practice for developing the correct techniques of goalkeeping.

Age Suitability

AGE	SUITABLE	COMMENTS
6-11	✗	Wait until children are 9 years old before using this exercise. Substitute six shots with a Three-Shot Stop.
12-15	✔	Two sets of the full Six-Shot Stop with a 45-60 second rest period in between. Best conducted immediately after team practice.
16+	✔	Ideally, conduct this exercise two to three times a week as a "maintenance" program: three sets of Six-Shot Stop at each session.

Salmon Leap

Objectives

To give a keeper the opportunity of making a save when "caught" off the line with a dipping, floating shot.

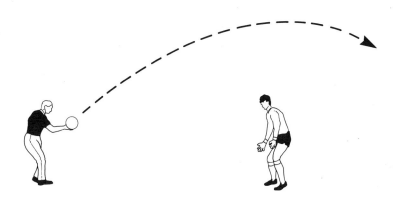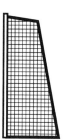

Organization

- Wherever possible use full-sized goals.

- Bring goalkeeper 5-6 yards off the goal line.

- The coach with a supply of balls is positioned 10-12 yards out.

- The goalkeeper must stand square to the coach and not anticipate the service.

- Six shots with the goalkeeper returning to the starting position — use two to three sets of 6 leaps.

- Give keeper enough time to recover to the "starting position" — otherwise will begin to "cheat."

Coaching Points

- The keeper should work hard to get back quickly without turning back on the ball.

- Develop judgment on whether to catch, push, or punch the ball over the bar, or to the side of the goal.

- When pushing ball over the bar, the keeper must work hard to give enough power to push the ball up and over.

- The final act of catching or pushing the ball may require a half turn towards the goal.

ABILITIES DEVELOPED	KC's EMPHASIZED
Quick footwork, power jumping and good decision making.	Alert and Alive, Stay On Feet, Open, Set.

ADDITIONAL INFORMATION

Even very good goalkeepers get caught off the goal line — sometimes it's through an error of judgment or the goalkeeper has done everything right in narrowing the angle, and the opponent produces a great chipped shot. Whatever, it happens. And frequently enough at every level to warrant regular practice.

A major and unique problem arises in these circumstances as the keeper moves quickly towards the goal. The final act — very often the dive or thrust for the ball — is accomplished by diving and falling back towards the goal. A normal contact — push or punch — on the ball may not be strong enough to take it up and over to safety. Therefore, a strong upward thrust is required (see illustration) with the momentum of the shot usually being sufficiently strong to carry the ball over and beyond the goal.

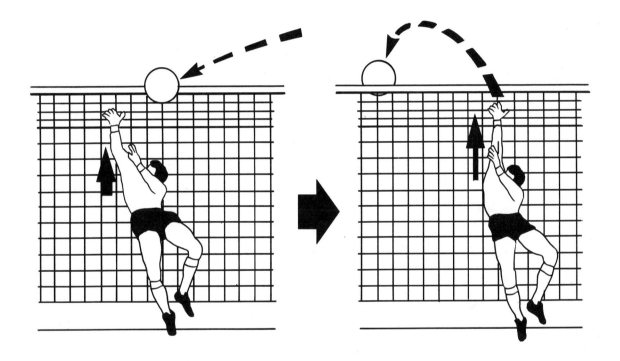

"Leaping Salmon" is what the goalkeepers must be. Make sure they practice this type of save often. Otherwise they may look like a fish out of water and make the coach look none-too-good at the same time.

Age Suitability

AGE	SUITABLE	COMMENTS
6-11	✗	Players at this age are not yet ready for this practice.
12-15	✔	Some time can be spent in this practice, but there are more important "basics" to be worked on.
16+	✔	Must be included on a regular basis in the practice program.

Wheeling and Dealing

Objectives

To develop throwing and kicking techniques; and accuracy of throwing and kicking.

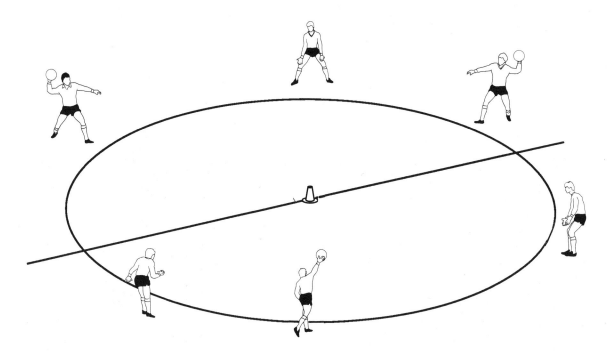

Organization

- If more than five goalkeepers are involved use a circle. If two, three or four keepers, use a square.

- A target (cone) is placed in the center of the area.

- The distances will depend on skills being developed.

- 10-yard radius for short throws and rolls.

- 15-yard radius for medium throws and accurate short goal kicks.

- 20 yards or more for longer throws and accurate kicks.

- Two can compete one against the other; or pairs can compete against each other; threes — one out winner stays in.

- Ensure the center is marked to reset the target when hit and knocked off center.

Coaching Points

- Encourage the kick or throw to reach the target as quickly as possible.

- Use "disguise" in dispatching the kick or throw to prevent anticipation by the opposition in game play.

- Over longer distances, encourage low trajectory throws to save time in the air, and to help "control" by receiver in game situations.

- Do not let the practice go too long as techniques can become sloppy through arm/shoulder/leg fatigue.

ABILITIES DEVELOPED	KC's EMPHASIZED
Accurate and well weighted throws and kicks.	Non-specific to KC's.

ADDITIONAL INFORMATION

In the Team Practice, field players and goalkeepers can work on this practice together. Certain conditions should be put on the goalkeepers or field players to bring about parity. For instance, using a regular center circle as the area, the field players merely have to knock over the cone by using a side foot pass, while the goalkeepers must make a direct hit on the cone before the ball touches the ground. Or, if the radius of the circle was extended to 15-20 yards for low-drive practice for the field players, the goalkeepers could be moved a further 3-5 yards out for longer throwing practice (which is relatively easier than the accuracy required for low driving).

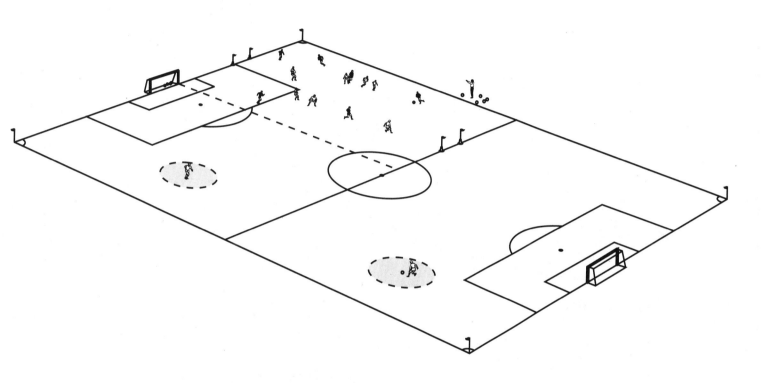

A goalkeeping pairs practice for goal kicking as a development of "Wheeling and Dealing" could be based on the practice below. Two zones are marked out with the goalkeepers kicking (from hands or on the ground) from one zone to the other. The ball must land within the zone to score a point.

Age Suitability

AGE	SUITABLE	COMMENTS
6-11	✔	Great for kicking and rolling the ball. Use a smaller radius for this age, e.g. 6-7 yards.
12-15	✔	Very applicable. Try to involve all the players together — field and goalkeeper.
16+	✔	Goalkeepers can work on own when field players are practicing specific skills, e.g. passing and support.

Criss-Cross

Objectives

To produce a high-activity drill giving repeated practice in the essential basic techniques of goalkeeping.

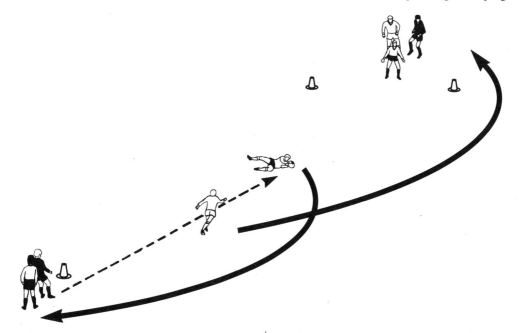

Organization

- A minimum of five, maximum of ten. Keepers split into two facing files at marker cones set 15/20 yards apart.

- The single-cone file act as the "servers"; the two-cone goal file the "goalkeepers."

- After each "serve" and each act of "goalkeeping" the players criss-cross to the end of the opposite file.

- Type of service to the "goalkeeper" can be changed periodically:

   Rolled ball for "collection."

   Rolled to side for diving save.

   Drop-kick service — less predictable.

   High-ball service.

   Short, diagonal roll — for diving at feet.

- After successfully collecting the ball the "keeper" projects a short, sharp, strong throw aimed at the chest of the waiting server.

Coaching Points

- Insist on high quality work at all times — even with the simplest of saves.

- The throw into the chest of the server is very important — encourage the ball to be "thumped" into the chest.

- While the goalkeeper must be "perfect," the oncoming player — the server on the criss-cross — should take avoiding action in injury-threatening situations.

- Coach should continuously reinforce the KC's — particularly the "Hands as the Leaders," and the "Open/Side Diving" considerations.

ABILITIES DEVELOPED	KC's EMPHASIZED
Good, sound technical habits.	Hands, Open, Alert and Alive, Side Diving, Absorption, AMOB III.

ADDITIONAL INFORMATION

The Criss-Cross practice can be adjusted to accommodate field players, with another set of conditions placed on the field players to emphasize passing and control, while retaining the goalkeeping practice for the keeper.

The Criss-Cross practice needs some modification for Cross Ball techniques.

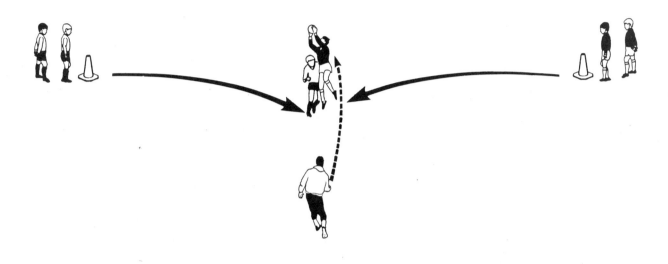

Instead of the keeper throwing the ball to the next "server," the ball is lobbed by the coach or "server" at the side. The criss-cross action continues. The incoming "attacker" should attempt to get across the "goalkeeper" to distract the keeper — or even make contact with the ball (without risking injury).

Great encouragement should be given to the goalkeepers in the Criss-Cross crossing to leap and to take the ball as high as possible, even if this results in the occasional mistake or misjudgment. The goalkeeper will get the feeling of "soaring" while collecting the ball (in match play the "soaring goalkeeper" can be inspirational to his/her own teammates — and demoralizing to the opposition).

Age Suitability

AGE	SUITABLE	COMMENTS
6-11	✔	An ideal way to introduce elements of goalkeeping technique.
12-15	✔	Excellent introductory warm-up drill for a goalkeeper clinic or team practice.
16+	✔	Worth adjusting the exercise for field players and goalkeepers because of the benefits.

Submarining

Objectives

To give goalkeeper practice in acquiring the correct "diving at the feet" techniques.

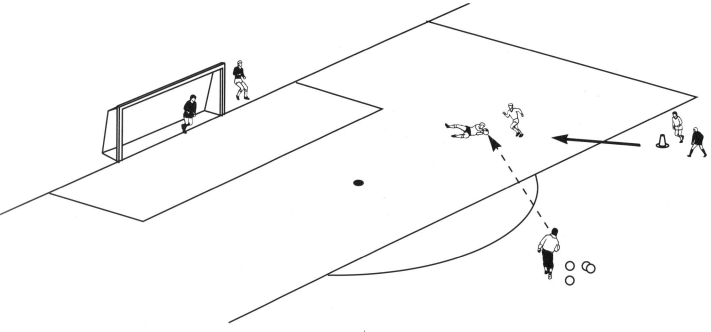

Organization

- "Shooters" line up as shown in illustration.

- "Server" is positioned behind the front players. Practice from right and later switch to left.

- Ball is rolled or passed by the server, but is biased for the goalkeeper. If 50/50 balls are served the "shooter" must take evasive action if any chance of injury.

- Use "criss-cross" principle of changing positions.

- Don't allow the "goalkeepers" to "cheat" by moving off their line too far, too early.

Coaching Points

- Keepers must be on their toes — **ready!**

- Goalkeepers must come out low — and fast — and, like the submariner, dive, dive, dive!

- As the practice is geared for technique work, it should result in a dive for the ball, in which case the keeper should be encouraged to:

  Go down a fraction early and "slide" into the side-diving position. A late dive could result in ball being played under body.

  Keep hands (towards ball) and head covering the near post; body and legs spreading to side, covering goal and far post.

  Don't allow keepers to "corkscrew" by coming out and turning inside-out so legs cover near post.

ABILITIES DEVELOPED	KC's EMPHASIZED
Correct at-the-feet Side Diving techniques.	Open, Side Diving, Hands, Don't Fall Back, Shape.

ADDITIONAL INFORMATION

Generally speaking, goalkeepers stay free of injury and play longer than field players. The physical demands of goalkeeping are not as great as field players. Staying injury free gives soccer longevity. Diving at the feet of on-rushing opponents is probably the most hazardous situation in goalkeeping.

Ironically, almost all severe injuries to goalkeepers in these situations come as a result of poor techniques. That is why it is critically important to work on this type of practice with young — and not-so-young — goalkeepers. Often young, inexperienced goalkeepers move out to deal with through balls, and kneel down to collect the ball, presenting the possibility of being kicked or kneed — usually on the head.

All the things we have stressed in the "Key Considerations" come into play in these kinds of situations in order to give the correct and safe method of diving at the feet, e.g.:

> The dive is on the side, with the hands going to the ball to give protection as a buffer to an attacker kicking through the ball.

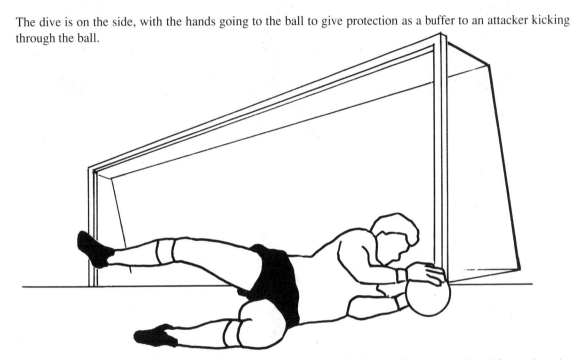

The goalkeeper must not fall backwards and slide legs out; nor swing the legs and knees around and forward on the dive and slide. All will produce ineffective goalkeeping, and could result in serious injury.

The simple rule is — hands and head to the ball — covering the near post; body and legs spread across — covering center goal and far post areas.

Age Suitability

AGE	SUITABLE	COMMENTS
6-11	✔	Essential practice for 9, 10 and 11 year olds, but must be strictly controlled to avoid any misunderstandings. Start with a gentle service without opposition.
12-15	✔	Avoidance of this type of practice will produce injuries in match play.
16+	✔	Good warm-up technique practice prior to more judgmental practice situations.

Let's Dance

Objectives

A warm-up and fitness exercise for goalkeepers concentrating on footwork.

Organization

- Depending on numbers, place one, two or three markers 6 yards apart and put "players" in line with 3 yards distance between players front to back.

- Leader takes a front position; is the "mirror" to which all others must respond.

- The "players" do everything that the "leader" does but in reverse to reflect the leader's actions.

- Keep the routine going for 12 minutes.

Coaching Points

- All movements forward, backward and sideways must be goalkeeper-style with shoulders to the ball (the leader).

- Leader should vary movements and speed of movement to keep "players" on their toes and reacting quickly.

- See Page 92 referring to goalkeeper movements across goal.

ABILITIES DEVELOPED	KC's EMPHASIZED
Goalkeeper endurance, balance and feet/body coordination.	Alert and Alive, Open, Shape.

ADDITIONAL INFORMATION

The Let's Dance routine can be performed by as few as two or as many as 200, all at the same time. It can — and on occasions should — be combined with the Shadow Goalkeeping outlined on the next page.

Although primarily designed for goalkeepers, there is no reason why "Let's Dance" should not involve the whole team. The Let's Dance routine is excellent for developing footwork whether a field player, tennis player, boxer — or dancer!

Two or three goalkeepers working together can go through the routine in isolation if the field players are practicing a more specific field-type activity, such as passing and control.

Twelve minutes is the recommended time for accomplishing the goalkeeping endurance requirement. It is the equivalent of the field players' *Cooper Run*.

With young goalkeepers under 14 years of age, don't be surprised if they are "distressed" after 3-6 minutes. All the more reason to implement this exercise on a regular basis. The inability to stay "Alert and Alive" and "Dancing" throughout the game is a negative characteristic of younger goalkeepers.

Age Suitability

AGE	SUITABLE	COMMENTS
6-11	✔	Do not use for 12 minutes — 3-4 minutes will be ample.
12-15	✔	Involve all players occasionally; 6 minutes with all the players; 12 minutes with goalkeepers only.
16+	✔	Essential warm-up and fitness activity for goalkeepers — with or without supervision.

Shadow Goalkeeping

Objectives

To replicate diving techniques and "saves" followed by fast "recovery" back to the feet.

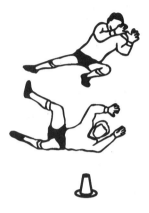   

Organization

- Either on own, with a partner, or with several goal-keepers arranged in files (see illustration).

- On own—use imagination to create the "action" — for six different saves with fast recovery into "ready" position between each save.

- With two or more — one person (coach or partner as leader) work on four main types of saves, e.g.:

    Collapse for ground shot close to body.

    Low shot just inside the post.

    Parallel dive — for shot 2-3 feet high, just inside the post.

    Top corner of the net.

Coaching Points

- Fast recovery is critical.

- Allow just enough time for "recovery," but not too much before next "shot."

- Coach or partner "directs" the type of shot by pointing.

ABILITIES DEVELOPED	KC's EMPHASIZED
Correct diving techniques, reactions and strength, and speed of recovery.	Side Diving, Open, Recovery, Shape.

ADDITIONAL INFORMATION

When I was 16, I was still unable to dive correctly. When I dived, I dragged my feet, with the result that invariably… I belly-flopped! I knew what the problems were, but I could not correct them, and I didn't have a coach.

Living by the seaside, with miles of sand and sand dunes, gave me the opportunity of practicing my goalkeeping dives anytime I wanted. So I devised my own Shadow Goalkeeping method. In my imagination I would replicate a series of shots on my goal and respond — physically. Without question, it helped me to develop my "side diving" techniques and my "recovery." As well, I won more games and brought the crowd to their feet far more times than I ever did in my 13-year professional career!

Imagery is one of the "tools" of skills learning today. But it does work and a goalkeeper can get 10 times the amount of "GK Saving Time" that he/she could ever get with a ball and a coach. Even better, you don't have the embarrassment of picking one single ball out of the back of the net!

Shadow Goalkeeping can be implemented within the "Let's Dance" routine — or for 3-5 minutes at the conclusion of the "Let's Dance" sequence.

If using as a separate or add-on exercise — do five sets of 6 "saves" — with 30-45 seconds of rest between each set.

Age Suitability

AGE	SUITABLE	COMMENTS
6-11	✔	Modified version with simple saves. Try the Mirror Man routine.
12-15	✔	Goalkeepers on a regular basis. Field players occasionally — for fun!
16+	✔	Two or three keepers can work together and use the Mirror Man method. Occasionally have the whole team go through the routine.

Mirror Man

Want some fun? Two goalkeepers (or field players) face one another. The players take it in turn performing any number of goalkeeper style actions (shadow form) with the other keeper trying to "mirror" every action simultaneously, or as near to simultaneously as possible. The same principle can be used with the field players, and they don't have to be soccer actions. Forward rolls, somersaults, back flips…you name it! Anything goes! It's great fun!

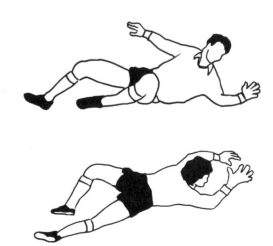

PRACTICES FOR COMBINED SKILLS

Two Goal Practice

Objectives

To receive repeated practice in shot-stopping techniques.

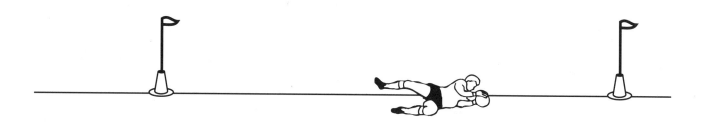

Organization

- Two goalkeepers work together.

- Goals are set up approx. 15-20 yards apart. Use portable goals, cones or corner flags.

- Service can be by throwing or kicking (including volleys and half volleys).

- Initially start by throwing the ball at one another; then vary service high and low, left and right. Objective should be to test and stretch one another rather than to score.

- Can be with or without supervision.

Coaching Points

- Alert and alive at all times — very much on toes.

- Aim for top quality work — even on simple stops.

- Always get as much body behind the ball as possible — even on simple saves.

- On partial saves, recover and respond quickly to complete the save.

ABILITIES DEVELOPED	KC's EMPHASIZED
Reactions, handling, footwork, diving and power diving.	Side Diving, Open, Stay On Feet, AMOB III, Set.

ADDITIONAL INFORMATION

For the youngest players (6-11 years) just catching a high ball is difficult enough. So set up the practice where the keepers are only 3 to 4 yards apart. Practicing a throw-in resulting in a high catch for the receiver is a good place to start (see Page 15).

Catch & Hug

Before moving into the two goal practice, the Under 12's should start with the Pendulum Roll and the Squat Thrust (Pages 40&41).

At the other end of the spectrum, the 16+ goalkeepers should be really testing one another with hard shots, deceptive lobs, balls rolled with pace into the corners — always giving the other keeper a chance, but at the same time making it difficult and challenging.

Age Suitability

AGE	SUITABLE	COMMENTS
6-11	✔	Modified Service. Mainly catching and throwing. Have goals only 5 to 6 yards apart — 3 to 4 yards wide at age 6, 7. Increase distances between players and width of goals with age.
12-15	✔	Excellent basic practice for goalkeepers. Can be done with or without supervision — perhaps when team is practicing for non-goalkeeping activities such as passing and support.
16+	✔	Essential basic "maintenance" practice. Now "permanent" positions have been established, the two (or three) Team Keepers should spend a large percentage of practice time (20%) in this type of situation.

Gone Fishing

Objectives

To gain an understanding of the timing and movement out of goal, and the angles required when advancing off the goal line to deal with an impending shot.

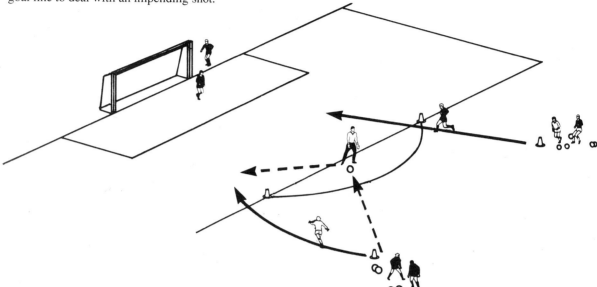

Organization

- Place markers as shown in the illustration.

- Make sure the markers on the penalty box are no more than goal width apart.

- One goalkeeper in goal, the other(s) waiting their turn. Change the goalkeeper every four to five shots.

- Field players equally divided between the two far markers. Field players should alternate their starting position (left/right).

- One player with a ball (does not matter from which side) plays into server, and ball is set up for shot either side.

- If played back outside the penalty area, two touches only; if inside the penalty area, must be shot first time.

- The shooter must always move into penalty area around outside of the marker. The non-shooting player can make any type of run — inside the marker if so desired — looking for rebound goal.

Coaching Points

- Goalkeeper must make quick decisions — to go all the way; or to simply narrow the angle.

- Encourage the goalkeeper to get "set" and "stay on the feet" just before the shot (if not diving at feet).

- Good body "shape" and "not falling backwards" are the two most important factors.

- Encourage shooter to shoot low across the goalkeeper towards far post.

- Rebound player must time run to arrive as ball comes off the goalkeeper.

ABILITIES DEVELOPED	KC's EMPHASIZED
Judgment in when to come off the line and how far, decision making of staying on feet, or "spreading."	React, Stay On Feet, Don't Fall Back, Set, Recovery, AMOB III.

ADDITIONAL INFORMATION

With the number of KC's highlighted by this particular practice, it becomes obvious this is a very important situation for goalkeepers to be placed in. It cannot be stressed strongly enough how beneficial this practice is. A great advantage from the coach's perspective, is that the shooting practice for the field players is equally as beneficial.

Once the goalkeepers become accustomed to the practice, they come to terms with the highly intimidating situation they face. Or to put it another way, once the goalkeepers start keeping their nerve, the shooters will have to produce high-quality skill to score. If the goalkeepers take up and hold good positions, their reactions, even their bodies, will prevent goals.

Field players must keep the ball low if the goalkeeper is performing skilfully. The low ball is the most difficult to save. As well, the ball across the goalkeeper inside the far post is the most difficult to react to. It requires diving back across the line of advancement.

If a goalkeeper is beaten by a shot at the near post side the keeper is to a greater or lesser extent, at fault (but don't be too severe with young keepers). It is not as bad when beaten by a far post shot.

Also remember, even though the goalkeepers can make it extremely difficult for the shooters, the field players should be scoring 30% - 50% of the time (but they probably won't if the keepers implement the KC's and judge the distance they should be advancing off the line).

Age Suitability

AGE	SUITABLE	COMMENTS
6-11	✗	Too advanced a practice for this age group.
12-15	✔	Good practice, though keepers at this age will find this practice quite difficult.
16+	✔	Very important practice for goalkeepers at this stage in their development. Should be used as often as possible.

Through Balls

Objectives

Realistic practice for goalkeepers in judging when and when not to move off the line for through balls; 1 vs. 1 work for field players.

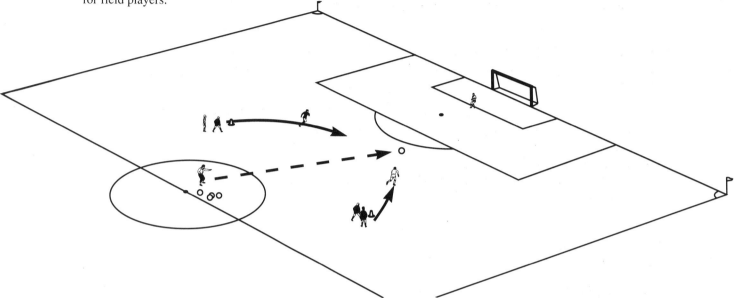

Organization

- Set up two groups of field players as above. Alternate the players after each attack to opposite file (left/right).

- Goalkeepers rotate after each shot.

- After an attack, give time to clear the area before serving the ball for next two players.

- Coach always touches ball to side before playing the ball in to get everyone "ready" to respond.

- Coach/server should vary the service: sometimes biased in favor of goalkeeper; sometimes to a field player.

- Occasionally give a three-way "hospital pass," and a lobbed/bouncing service.

Coaching Points

- Starting position of the goalkeeper critical — off the line to gain yards, but not too far to be exposed to an accurate long chip ball.

- Early decision is desirable but exception to "good goalkeeping rules" can apply here:

  As ball is played in, goalkeeper can move forward two or three paces while still assessing the situation. If the decision is to "go" — then ground has already been gained. If decision is to stay, the keeper relaxes while skipping and dancing back to original starting position.

- See section on "Onion Rings" and goalkeeper position when "out of direct" action (Pages 88&89).

- Good decisions and good techniques for final action — diving at feet to win the ball; spreading and forcing attacker wide; or standing up and reacting to shot.

ABILITIES DEVELOPED	KC's EMPHASIZED
Judgment of how far and how fast to move out, narrowing angle, diving at feet, standing up.	Alert and Alive, Stay On Feet, Shape, Don't Fall Back, React.

ADDITIONAL INFORMATION

Too often "Through Ball" situations are ignored by coaches. Shooting and crossing practices form the bulk of "team practices" that involve goalkeeping. The judgment required by the goalkeeper in assessing whether to move off the line to narrow the angle, or to go "all the way"— within, or even outside the penalty box — is arguably the most difficult aspect of goalkeeping; even more so than dealing with crosses, which is a severe test of goalkeeping judgment. The perspective of a ball coming directly towards a person is much more difficult than getting "a fix" on a ball played across the goal from wing areas.

I've often likened the situation to that of being a car driver who pulls out to overtake a slower vehicle when, at the same moment, down the road, another car comes around a corner. How far away is the oncoming car? How fast is it travelling? What about the comparative speeds?

Although it may not be identical to a goalkeeping situation, the solution is usually the same — if you are not sure don't do it! Stay back in a safe position and protect yourself (and your goal).

A development of this Through Ball practice is to have the two players go from one side (the side to which the ball is played). The "inside" player of the two is the attacker, the outside player is the recovering defender. This is a very realistic situation for all players, and increases the critical judgment required by the goalkeeper.

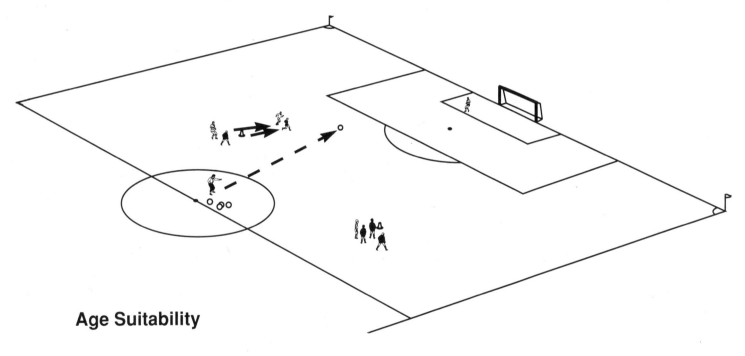

Age Suitability

AGE	SUITABLE	COMMENTS
6-11	✗	Young goalkeepers are not ready for this type of practicing yet, and a lack of judgment and technique could result in accidents.
12-15	✔	Excellent practice both for the goalkeeper and for attacker and defender in 1 vs 1 situations.
16+	✔	Apart from the skill practice for both goalkeeper and field players, this activity calls for hard running and persistence for the field player.

*Practice development suggested by Trevor Hartley, former coach of the Malaysian National Team and Tottenham Hotspur.

Diving Headers

Objectives

To present a challenging game requiring high-quality attacking heading; to place goalkeepers in situations requiring good assessment and reactions.

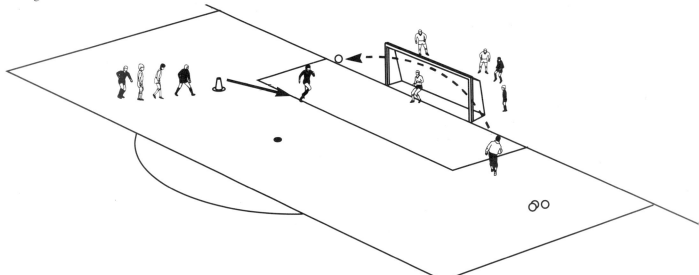

Organization

- Group is split in half with a recognized goalkeeper in each group.

- One group heads for goal; the other retrieves the balls — apart from the designated goalkeeper, who defends the goal.

- Ball is served by coach to produce "header" for goal — with a significant percentage of serves requiring a diving header.

- Goalkeeper does whatever is required to prevent the goal.

- Goalkeeper must return to near-post position after each serve — the server/coach can throw the ball directly into goal if the keeper anticipates the cross.

- Each team has a certain number of headers (e.g. 20) and then changes places with other group.

Coaching Points

- "Heading" group should be encouraged to head ball down and away from the keeper.

- The "header" back across the goalkeeper is particularly difficult for the keeper to deal with.

- Suggest the goalkeeper to hold near-post position until the server has committed a thrown ball across the goal.

- Advise keeper to move across goal quickly and, if possible get "set" for the header (time may not allow this).

- Encourage the goalkeeper to try to "read" the type of header — and then consider "playing the percentages" by sometimes "spreading."

ABILITIES DEVELOPED	KC's EMPHASIZED
For the keeper — good judgment, nerve and reactions.	Alert and Alive, Stay On Feet, Open, Don't Fall Back, Set.

ADDITIONAL INFORMATION

"Diving Headers" is a similar practice to Side Kicks, and puts the goalkeeper under the same type of decision-making pressure. "Know-how" and nerve are important here, because the odds are against the goalkeeper. Therefore, praise should be given for the good saves, even the near saves. Consideration and, where possible, encouragement should be exercised for the ones that get away. Too severe criticism could have a negative effect.

Once the goalkeeper realizes the requirements and begins to "play the percentages," the rewards can be significant.

This practice can be developed/progressed so that the service by foot and headers for goal are all performed by the players. Any goal counts, but a headed goal counts double. Make sure there is an opportunity to practice from both sides.

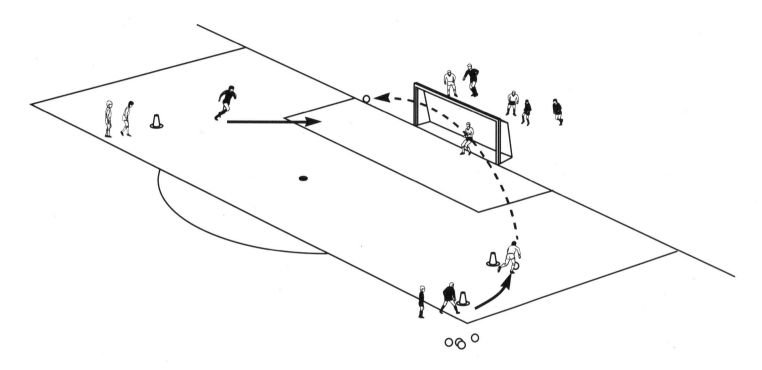

Age Suitability

AGE	SUITABLE	COMMENTS
6-11	✘	Not yet ready for this practice. Leave heading to next age phase.
12-15	✔	Excellent practice for this age group, but the heading standards will not be very good. Initially use an easy serve.
16+	✔	First class practice. At this age the players should be ready to progress to the "developed" practice outlined above.

Side Kicks

Objectives

To develop the understanding and the decision making involved in attacks from the sides of the goal; a meaningful practice for field players in clinical finishing.

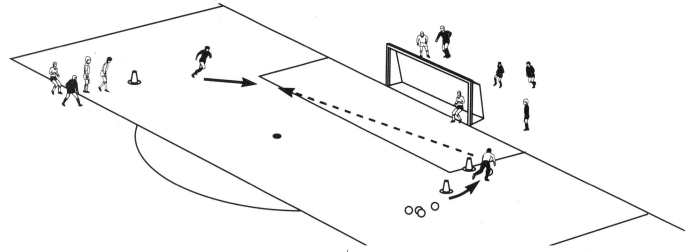

Organization

- Set out the penalty box as shown in the illustration. The practice starts from one side and is later changed to the other.

- Initially the "side kick" can be served in by the coach; later by the players.

- The keeper must start at the near post area. If the keeper "anticipates," the cross then shots/goals are permitted at the near post.

- The squad should be split into two teams — one shooting while the other "fields." The "challenge" is between the two teams.

- The goalkeepers have their own "challenge" — to keep the success rate on scoring under 50%.

- It is important that the placement of the cones is such that the cone nearest the goal line for the "side kick" is sufficiently close to the end line to make the cross a "pull-back."

Coaching Points

- Goalkeepers must defend the near post — first and foremost.

- Encourage goalkeepers to position marginally in front of the near post — so they won't push a high shot into the top of the net, nor crash into the post. They may consider using the hand extended sideways and backwards to touch the post.

- After forcing the cross by holding position, the keeper can cut out the cross ball — or, more likely, move across the goal to defend the impending shot.

- As ball is played across the goal, the keeper must move towards the far post fast, and attempt to "set" just before the shot.

- If there is a delay in the shot, it may be possible to advance a step or two to cut down the angle.

- Praise each keeper for every effort and success (there may not be too many to start with!).

ABILITIES DEVELOPED	KC's EMPHASIZED
The "nerve" and the "know how" to maximize the chances of saving.	Stay On Feet, React, Set, Don't Fall Back, Shape.

ADDITIONAL INFORMATION

As a progression, the players themselves can cross the ball and work on a rotation. Cross - Shoot - Cross, and so on. As well, the practice area can be extended to work on side crosses from further distances out.

The decision and action process that takes place for the goalkeeper is as follows:

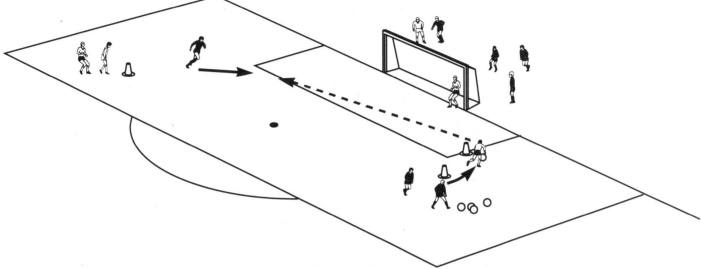

1. Hold near post position, face up to the ball. Do not allow near-post goal.

2. As the ball is crossed, can I hold or deflect the ball by diving out, or

3. Can I get across my goal, check my run and face up for the shot?

4. If the striker is delaying the shot, for whatever reason, can I get "set" in case the shot is played across the body.

5. If the cross is slow, can I get into position and move out a pace or two, or

6. If the cross is fast, and the shooter is committed to steer the ball into the ball into the corner, "gamble" by diving and spreading?*

*This is not "anticipation" — it's a "last ditch" calculated gamble.

Age Suitability

AGE	SUITABLE	COMMENTS
6-11	✘	Not ready for this yet.
12-15	✔	Best with the coach as the "side kick" server — therefore controlling the situation.
16+	✔	Excellent for goalkeeper and team — with a good chance of goalkeepers being pleasantly surprised by their success rate.

Goalie Shootout

Objectives

To present a challenging situation that demands high caliber shot stopping and accuracy of kicking and throwing.

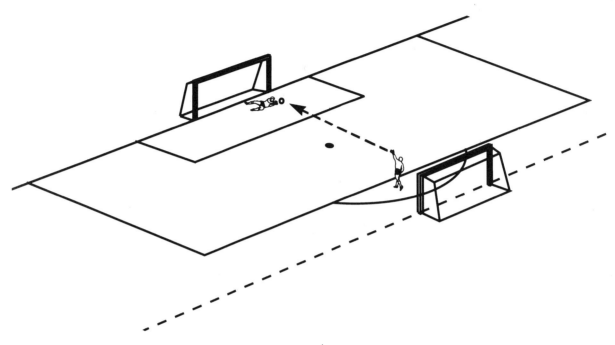

Organization

- Set up two goals 24 yards apart — if a portable goal is not available use corner flags 8 yards apart for one goal and a fixed goal as the other.

- A 6-yard line is put in front of each goal.

- Neither goalkeeper can come in advance of the 6-yard line either to shoot or to save.

- The "shooting" keeper has the choice of throwing, punting, drop kicking or shooting from the ground to score.

- For younger goalkeepers it will be necessary to shorten the distances between the goals (20/22 yards).

- First keeper to score 5 (or 8, or 10, etc.) wins.

Coaching Points

- Throwing will give the greatest accuracy and should be encouraged — although throwing is more predictable and not as powerful as kicking.

- Encourage the punt shot as well, as this can be powerful and less predictable as it often dips.

- The half-volley kick is probably the most powerful, but usually the least consistent. To give practice in the drop kick however, condition one of the "Shoot-outs" to be drop kicks only.

- Encourage keepers to read type of shot coming in. For instance with a lobbed throw the keeper must stay near goal line; with a half-volley kick the keeper can quickly move out a step or two to narrow the angle.

ABILITIES DEVELOPED	KC's EMPHASIZED
Good throwing and kicking techniques; shot stopping abilities.	Alert and Alive, Hands, Side Diving, Shape, Set.

ADDITIONAL INFORMATION

The availability, or rather the non-availability, of the right type of equipment and facilities will always be a headache to coaches. The chance of having portable goals here, there and everywhere is extremely unlikely, so improvisation has to be the key to this type of practice situation.

It has already been suggested that a goal made of corner flags can be set up 6 yards outside the penalty area of a regulation field.

Alternatively, to retain realism and authenticity, goalkeepers can take turns using one regulation sized goal. Five shots each and then switch, using the existing field markings and the 18-yard line as the limit for shooting.

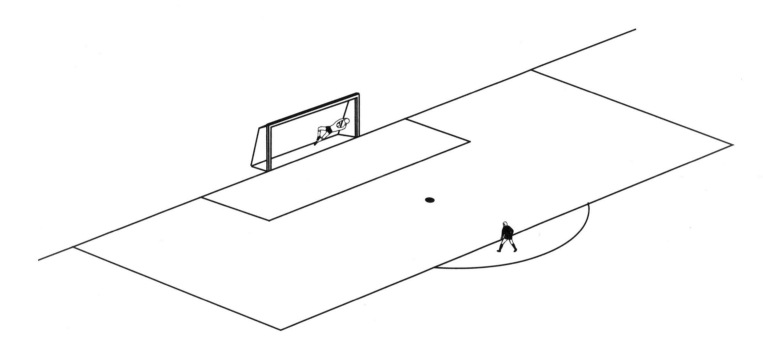

Age Suitability

AGE	SUITABLE	COMMENTS
6-11	✗	Not ready for this yet.
12-15	✔	Good practice except that regulation goals may still be too big for many goalkeepers at this age. Score 3 points for a goal below head height, 1 point for a goal above head height.
16+	✔	Very challenging situation for team goalkeepers, where they can practice with minimal supervision.

HANDS, KNEES AND BUMPS-A-DAISY!

If it were medically possible, all would-be goalkeepers should have their knees removed at birth and so prevent them getting in the way later on!

The worst goalkeeper sight to behold during the beginner phase is the keeper bending down with both kneecaps protruding, where the "knees" become the leaders not the hands.

The old song used to say "Hands, Knees, and Bumps-a-Daisy." That is not as bad as "Knees, Hands and it Bumps away!"

So if doctors are not able to cooperate then the goalkeeper must remove the offending part of the body — the knees — from contact with the ball.

This can be accomplished by:

1. Making sure the hands are kept well in front of the legs — particularly on low shots that are being collected.

2. When bending down to collect a low ball either by turning the knees to one side (the keeper may look like Quasimodo, but it works) or by keeping the knees as far back as possible by bending the body forward of the legs.

Please note: Turning the knees to the side still requires the upper body and shoulders to be square to the ball. And the knees, although turned out to the side, can and should still be used for double cover (see AMOB III).

GAME DECISION SITUATIONS

Near & Far

Objectives

A team practice to encourage good crossing techniques; timing of runs to near and far post; for goalkeepers — decision making and practice in cross ball situations.

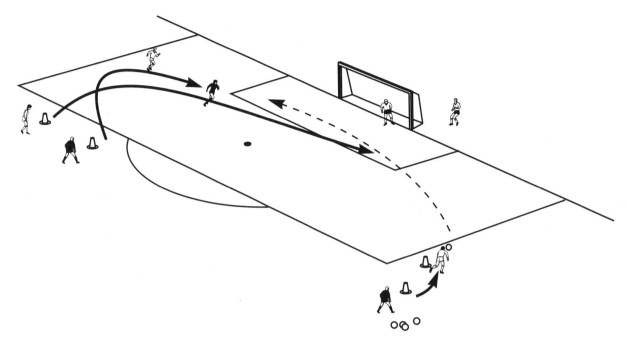

Organization

- Split field players into three equal groups as shown above.

- Goalkeepers (usually two or three) rotate after each cross.

- Players in wide positions start with ball at back cone; must play ball forward beyond front cone and then cross (two touches).

- Twin strikers on other side of penalty area move off their cones and decide who attacks which space.

- After each cross the field players rotate their positions.

- Practice area should be switched periodically so crosses come in from other side.

Coaching Points

- Encourage and teach good quality crosses into the near and far post areas; good quality timing of runs and execution of the shots by the strikers.

- Goalkeepers must appreciate the best starting positions to attack crosses to near and far post; must not be scored on by mis hit cross.

- Decision making by goalkeeper is critical — early decision and action (or hold position); must "play the percentages."

- Encourage the goalkeepers to call when coming out, e.g. "Keeper!"

ABILITIES DEVELOPED	KC's EMPHASIZED
Judgment of when and when not to attack a cross, and when to catch/when to punch.	Alert and Alive, Open, Absorption, Recovery.

ADDITIONAL INFORMATION

As the players become familiar with the practice and become more accomplished, a cooperating defender can be introduced to help the goalkeeper. The communication, with the goalkeeper in the dominant "see-all" role, is critically important.

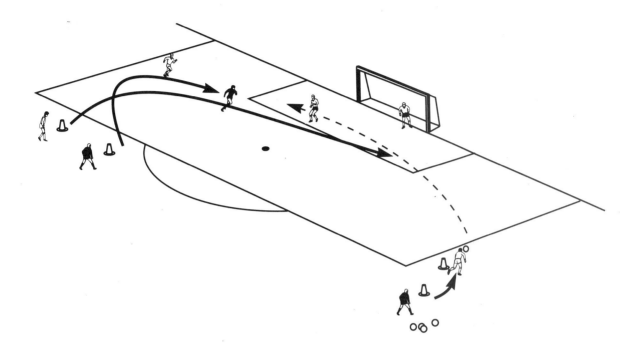

Obviously this practice can be developed and progressed (see Crossroads on next page) in all kinds of ways — by adding attackers and defenders. However, do not feel that adding numbers is necessarily a "progression." This practice in it's simplest form will be challenging to every player involved.

Age Suitability

AGE	SUITABLE	COMMENTS
6-11	✘	Not yet capable of the sophistication of this type of practice.
12-15	✔	Strongly recommended for this age group.
16+	✔	Strongly recommended. Consider bringing in a supporting defender at some stage.

Crossroads

Objectives

To give team practice in crossing; timing of runs; realistic shooting and heading; goalkeepers — realistic cross ball situations.

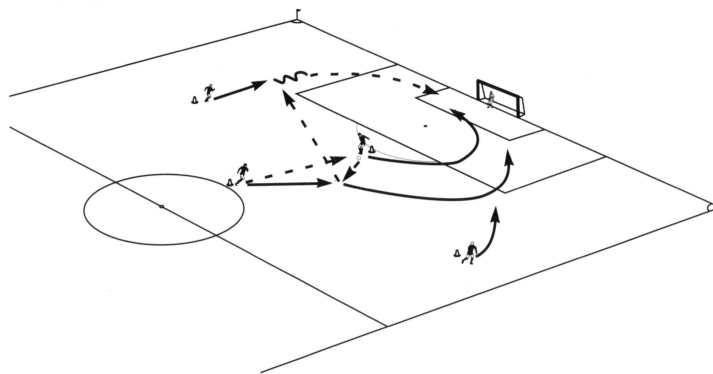

Organization

- Distances/positions of the four starting stations can be varied according to age/ability of players but should be similar to above.

- Field players are divided equally between the four starting positions (not shown in illustration).

- Good quality passing, setting up play, diagonal pass and crossing is essential.

- Goalkeepers (two or three) can rotate in goal after each 3 or 4 crosses.

- Coach must ensure the practice area is clear before allowing the next attacking wave.

- A single defender can be added if the practice begins to work successfully.

Coaching Points

- Insist on high standards of passing/crossing from field players.

- Encourage goalkeeper to be acutely aware of starting position and adjustment as attack develops.

- Point out the necessity for good, early decisions and if necessary, action.

- Ask the goalkeeper to establish the habit of communicating the decision loudly and early, even when not coming for the ball ("Away!").

ABILITIES DEVELOPED	KC's EMPHASIZED
Judgment of when/when not to come for cross; when/when not to catch or punch.	Alert and Alive, Open, Absorption, React, Recovery.

ADDITIONAL INFORMATION

A high percentage of goals (70%+) are scored from attacks initiated from crosses and passes played in from the flank areas. While it was stated earlier that judgment of through balls is probably the most difficult situation a goalkeeper faces, the fact is a keeper will deal with many more cross ball situations than through ball situations. A "final judgment" on the ability of keepers is usually made on their skill at dealing with crosses. At the risk of being called sexist, cross ball situations "sort out the men from the boys" in goalkeeping.

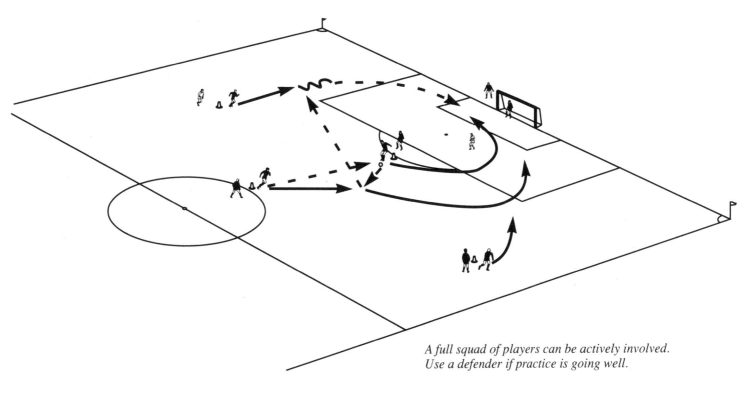

A full squad of players can be actively involved. Use a defender if practice is going well.

Therefore, no opportunity should be lost to gain practice in these types of situations. Also, any coach ignoring the importance of cross-ball practice and denying his/her team the opportunity of practicing in these circumstances is failing to coach the game of soccer.

The Crossroads practice is a challenging one, but is very enjoyable. Players will be highly motivated in these situations.

Age Suitability

AGE	SUITABLE	COMMENTS
6-11	✘	Too advanced for this age group.
12-15	✔	Very good practice but have starting positions nearer to goal and not too wide.
16+	✔	First class practice — a defender can be introduced after a while to help the keepers.

GK's Chip 'n Dale

Objectives

To produce a team practice emphasizing good collective defending and attacking, with the goalkeepers acting as the supporters of attackers, and initiators of scoring opportunities.

Organization

- Mark out area approx. 35 x 40 yards.

- Two rectangular shaped zone boxes placed beyond each end line (approx. 5 yards away).

- Squad is split into two teams, and each team is halved — one half on the field, the other in the zone.

- Goals only count if ball is chipped forward, then caught in the end zone without touching the ground.

- Goalkeeper on each outside line is available to team in possession, and can receive the pass, but must throw back to same team.

- Keepers can throw ball to one another across the area to help create space for team in possession.

Coaching Points

- See "Coaching the Team" manual for field players coaching points.

- Encourage goalkeepers to dance along their sidelines always facing the play/always available.

- Instruct goalkeepers to communicate their availability (or non-availability) to the player in possession.

- Encourage quick-thinking decisions by the keepers after receiving the ball.

- If a good "pass" is not on for the keeper, the point of possession should be changed by a fast, accurate, non-interceptable throw to other keeper.

ABILITIES DEVELOPED	KC's EMPHASIZED
Good decision making, and accurate use of the ball; good throwing techniques.	Alert and Alive, Hands, Open.

ADDITIONAL INFORMATION

While this practice was designed principally for the field players, this is another example of a meaningful practice for all of the team, where the goalkeepers practice and cooperate with their teammates in situations that develop good team understanding. Too often, as has been emphasized elsewhere in this book, goalkeepers spend practice time on technique and in non-thinking situations and on their own. Coaches are then surprised when their keepers cannot successfully apply these techniques in the game because the decision-making process (e.g. when cooperating with their teammates) lets them down.

Age Suitability

AGE	SUITABLE	COMMENTS
6-11	✗	Too complex a practice for this age — but Chip 'n Dale without the goalkeepers will be fine for 9, 10 and 11 year olds.
12-15	✔	First class practice for all players. Initially don't expect standards to be very high.
16+	✔	Highly recommended team practice to develop collective attacking and defending.

Mixed Bag

Objectives

To place goalkeepers (and field players) in decision-making situations with attacks developed from the wings.

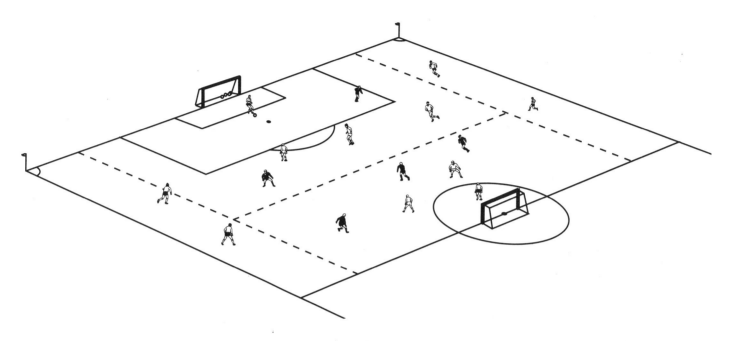

Organization

- Use half of a full-sized field; mark out an 8-yard channel each side of field

- Mark in a half-way line; 3 vs 2 and a goalkeeper in each half.

- The channelled wingers have no allegiance — they play for both teams.

- When ball is in hands of keeper, and when restarting play, goalkeeper always throws to flank players of the keeper's choice.

- Wing players can pass to one another, overlap, and cross the ball; can play ball in/out to the three attackers.

- Change around the players periodically to give experience in the different roles (except goalkeepers).

Coaching Points

- Goalkeepers must work on accurate throws to wide players.

- Goalkeepers should be encouraged to "switch" play.

- Keepers must communicate their requirements and organize the defence.

- The goalkeepers must observe the changing circumstances, adjust accordingly and take the required action.

- Field players: encourage good attacking runs (near and far post); timing of runs of players from defending positions; skilful cooperative defending against greater numbers (3 vs 2).

ABILITIES DEVELOPED	KC's EMPHASIZED
Judgment and decision making in relation to cross ball situations.	Alert and Alive, Open, Stay On Feet, Hands.

ADDITIONAL INFORMATION

Practice can begin with simpler numbers. For instance, 2 vs 1 in each half; only one flank player. Then player numbers can be built up to the type of situation shown on the opposite page.

As the coach and the players become familiar with this type of practice — it will take several weeks — the practice can be further developed where, for instance:

Defenders can play the ball directly in to front attacking players without the ball having to go wide.

A defender can be released to go forward over the half-way line to support an attack.

One defender and one attacker can go into the other half to assist play (players own choice), but have to get back quickly when ball goes to goalkeeper.

One of the flank players can follow pass or cross to assist the attacking team.

These alternatives really do produce the "Mixed Bag" circumstances which further extend the judgment and decision making for the goalkeepers.

Age Suitability

AGE	SUITABLE	COMMENTS
6-11	✘	Too advanced for the age
12-15	✔	Better to keep the numbers small, e.g. 2 vs 1, and not progress the practice or increase the numbers too quickly.
16+	✔	Extremely demanding for goalkeepers, but enjoyable and challenging for all players.

GK Ball

Objectives

Fun game giving good practice in heading, volleying, supporting play and appreciation of space for field players; for goalkeepers — opportunity of developing throwing, catching and shot-stopping techniques.

Organization

- Work in an area 30 x 35 yds. approx. with full sized goals for players 13 years and older.

- Improvise goals if two full sized goals are not available.

- Ball can only be moved by throwing to teammate. Players cannot run with the ball. All passes must be caught before touching the ground.

- Goals can be scored from a throw to a teammate to head or volley into the net. The ball must not touch the ground before entering the goal.

- Interceptions can be made by opposition; everyone can use their hands. Opposition gets possession if ball hits ground.

- Partial interceptions can be disputed and claimed by either side by diving on the ball.

Coaching Points

- Team in possession must support well.

- Far post positions essential for scoring opportunities.

- Near and far-post runs cause confusion to defending team.

- Headers easier to score than volleys.

- Goalkeepers should always recover quickly to own goal after team loses possession, as they will be key players on the goal line.

ABILITIES DEVELOPED	KC's EMPHASIZED
Good all-round decision making.	All in a general way.

ADDITIONAL INFORMATION

While this is mainly a "diversionary" type of practice, it not only produces enjoyment, it encourages good team play, supporting play and develops an understanding of attacking awareness.

From the goalkeeper's perspective, the major benefit besides the goal mouth situations, is in the collection and use of the ball. Too often when goalkeepers collect the ball in a game they are indecisive. Should they kick or throw the ball quickly? Usually, because of their indecision, they "freeze" and nothing happens (except they may incur the displeasure of their teammates not to mention the coach!). Even worse, on certain occasions they can panic and on the spur of the moment throw or roll a risky pass to a player or area close to their goal.

Being comfortable with the ball in the hands, secure in the knowledge they have the ability to use the ball if they so decide, but composed enough to take their time if they choose to do so, helps the all-round goalkeeping performance.

The GK Ball can be a first class game at a training camp, soccer school or goalkeeping academy when there is more time than the usual team practice allows.

Age Suitability

AGE	SUITABLE	COMMENTS
6-11	✔	Play with small numbers, two games if necessary, on a small field.
12-15	✔	Good way to start the practice. Do some stretching exercises before commencing.
16+	✔	As for the 12-15. Use as warm-up preceded by stretching.

No Sleeper Keeper

Objectives

To place all players (goalkeepers and field players) in a fun game situation giving practice in collective team play and decision-making situations; produces "reaction save" and "use of the ball" circumstances.

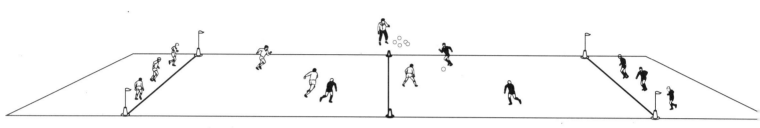

Organization

- A 20 x 10 yard area is marked with corner flags and half way line markers (cones); a 5-yard end zone is added.

- Each team is split — three goalkeepers, two midfielders and one forward, and restricted to their "zone." Only goalkeepers can use their hands.

- Keepers are not allowed beyond their end zone, but must defend both the "goal" and the zone.

- Goals can be scored in the following ways:

  1. Goalkeepers shooting, throwing or punting through the goals; or throwing, punting, chipping to land ball in opposite end zone.

  2. Midfielders shooting through goals (or chipping into end zone).

  3. Forwards can shoot or pick up rebounds to score.

4. Game is always restarted after ball goes out of play by a goalkeeper of team which did not touch the ball last.

Coaching Points

- Encourage good organization/communication/decision making by the "goalkeepers."

- Look for quick decisions by goalkeepers when gaining possession to see if a throw or lob can catch out opposition.

- Encourage midfielders to look for quick shots or chips; also to maintain possession (2 vs 1) when shot not possible.

- Advise attackers to be always gambling for rebounds; also positioning for build-up play from goalkeepers and midfielders.

ABILITIES DEVELOPED	KC's EMPHASIZED
Awareness and decision making in quickly changing situations.	Alert and Alive, React, Open.

ADDITIONAL INFORMATION

If the ball is chipped or thrown into the end zone the "zone" can be defended by the goalkeepers catching the ball before it hits the ground, trapping the ball with the hands as it hits the ground (providing it doesn't bounce or squirm away), or by tipping or punching the ball out of the sides of the zone without the ball touching the ground. Note: it cannot be tipped or punched over the end line — no matter how high (penalty: a goal to the other side).

The "No Sleeper Keeper" game was developed by former Glasgow Rangers player and USYSA Coach, Billy McNichol and his wife, Stacey. It's a fun, action-packed game requiring all players to develop "knowse" — better defined as awareness, alertness and craftiness! This "game savvy" helps players when placed in demanding quick decision game situations.

The game can be modified for team practice to keep regular goalkeepers permanently in goal. Alternatively, it can be used at goalkeeper clinics and goalkeeper schools as a Team Goalie Game.

Age Suitability

AGE	SUITABLE	COMMENTS
6-11	✔	The game can be modified to make it a throw and catch only game with the throw and catch replacing the foot passing.
12-15	✔	Good game for all young soccer players and helps develop a better team understanding.
16+	✔	Top rate game for mature players.

Super 8's

Objectives

To produce a fast-changing soccer game with most of the critical decision-making ingredients of 11-a-side play, including offside; to provide realistic game development opportunities for goalkeepers.

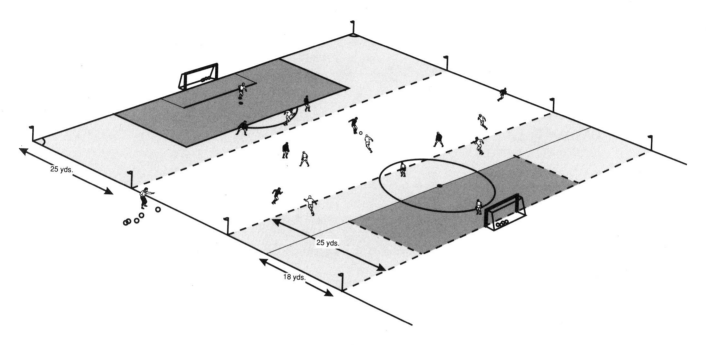

Organization

- Set up a line and regulation sized goal 18 yards beyond center line. If a portable goal is not available use corner flags.

- Mark in two 25-yard lines with coaching disks — if available use corner flags to emphasize 25-yard lines.

- If available use two people — assistant coaches, parents, to act as linesmen, stationed on opposite sides of field to coach at the 25-yard lines.

- Normal rules of soccer, except that each team can only be offside beyond attacking 25-yard lines.

- Consider narrowing field by 5 to 10 yards on each side if regulation width (i.e. 74 yards).

Coaching Points

- Encourage goalkeepers to organize rear players to "utilize" offside to keep opponents away from goal.

- Encourage "total soccer" with players moving up and down field with no set positions; therefore playing "both ways."

- Good communication from the keepers is important. Encourage keepers to be "on their toes" as situations change and develop very quickly.

- Encourage awareness, attacking support, width and defensive cover.

- Encourage goalkeepers to help "organize" the team.

ABILITIES DEVELOPED	KC's EMPHASIZED
This is a "putting it all together" practice covering most facets of goalkeeping.	All.

ADDITIONAL INFORMATION

Most teams have a roster of 14 to 18 players. While 11 vs 11 play can be advantageous in developing team understanding, most teams cannot organize "in-house" 11 vs 11 play...but can play 7 vs 7 or 8 vs 8.

8 vs 8, the "Super" game, produces most of the questions and answers required of 11-a-side play — particularly in match play when the "game plan" is not working, and players are forced to think for themselves.

"Super 7's" and "Super 9's" are quite acceptable, if there are too few or too many players.

The demanding nature of the Super 8's game will help develop the "two-way" player that is so desirable in modern-day soccer.

From the goalkeepers' perspective, because of the fast-changing end-to-end nature of the game, and with the "offside" rule in effect, most of the tough situations that face goalkeepers in the 11 vs. 11 game will occur here — through balls, cross balls, long shots, short range shots — except 10 times more action will happen here than in the normal full-sided game.

As well, the distribution of the ball by the keeper — by hand or foot — will be extremely testing due to the smaller field. For instance, a long kick will often end up in the other goalkeepers hands. So the alternative of a throw, in an attempt to help create an attack, will be preferable. But bad decisions and irresponsible throws will be punished.

Age Suitability

AGE	SUITABLE	COMMENTS
6-11	✔	Not recommended for practice situations, but a good match play format for 10-11 year olds.
12-15	✔	Good practice method. Should be used regularly.
16+	✔	Excellent practice method. Recommended for a significant percentage of practice time.

Big Shot

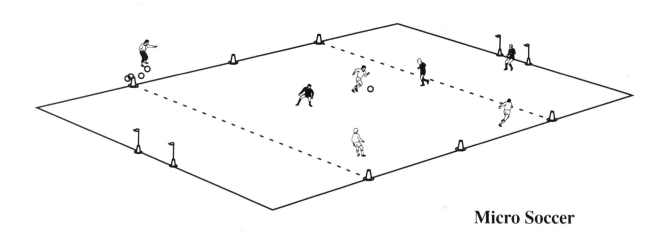

Micro Soccer

Attack vs Defense

For more information on these practices, see manual, *Coaching The Team*

PUTTING IT ALL TOGETHER

POSITIONAL PLAY

There is a vast difference between "anticipating" something that might happen as opposed to "reading" the game. When "reading" the game a goalkeeper will make decisions and move into position with the knowledge there is a greater percentage chance that the goal can be defended from that position and that his presence in that area will cause maximum discomfort to opponents — and the shooter in particular.

Onion Rings

Look at the illustration to see the numbered areas of goalkeeping.

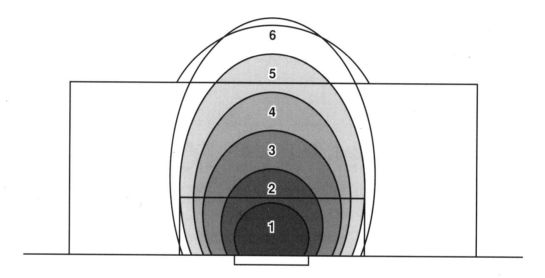

A goalkeeper who is good in Area 1, but poor in Area 6, may still be an outstanding goalkeeper.

A goalkeeper who is good in Area 6, but poor in Area 1, shouldn't be a goalkeeper! But would probably make an excellent defender.

A lot has been written and talked about in regard to "extending the range of the goalkeeper." All other things being equal (which they never are!) the ability to do well in Area 6 may be the difference between one very good goalkeeper and another.

The "Sweeper Keeper" role is an important consideration in goalkeeping today, and with the rules of the game being modified to compel the goalkeeper to become more of a "footballer," there is every reason for a keeper to work on foot skills, and this should be encouraged.

But charity, and good goalkeeping, begin at home. It is critical for the coach to recognize this, and to start from basics, and then move forward.

Basic Goalkeeping is the ability to prevent shots from entering the goal. Therefore, the basic goalkeeping position is on or near the goal line.

Position with the Ball Away From Goal

The illustration shows positions a goalkeeper should be encouraged to take up when the ball is away from the defending penalty area. As the play moves out, the goalkeeper is able to move out and push out the back players to support the midfield and front players, while always on the alert for a long penetrative clearance by the opposition.

The general rule is the keeper moves out as the play goes to the other end of the field. And moves back and adjusts position as the opposition build up play towards the goalkeeper's goal.

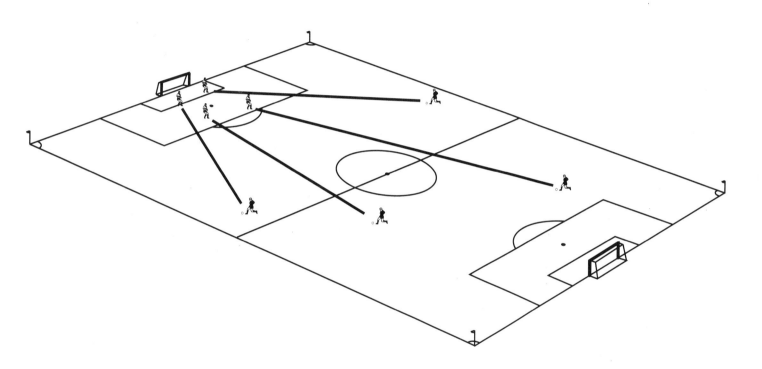

Even when moving (dancing!) back towards the goal, the keeper has no need to look backwards. The goals are fixed and don't move and the penalty area dimensions on regulation fields are the same the world over. Providing the field markings are distinct, the goalkeeper's position should be based upon a complete knowledge of the penalty area guided by the markings of the area, penalty spot, the "D" and the six yard box.

With practice and awareness, goalkeepers should know, almost within an inch and at a glance, just where they are in their area, without taking their attention away from play.

Beware the 35 Yard Line

One problem with the positional guideline given in the last illustration is that the "rule" changes when the ball comes to within 30 to 35 yards of goal. There may be the temptation for a goalkeeper to "steal" a few yards by holding at the 6-yard line on the retreat — or to move out to the 6-yard box as play moves out beyond the penalty box. Be warned! Be careful! A speculative blast at goal may appear to be a "long shot" but, as the power of the shot diminishes, it can dip at the last second, right under the crossbar. It happens too often to be dismissed as a fluke. If the keeper is caught off the line on a shot from 35 yards out, it is bad goalkeeping. The goalkeeper was in the wrong position.

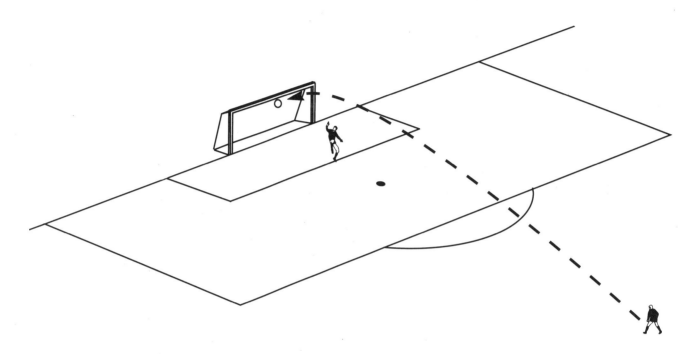

The other problem of being caught out of goal by a long shot, is the lack of a "reference frame" from which the keeper can make judgments. Caught in "no-man's land" may result in goalkeepers "waving" at shots above their heads. With the keeper back on the goal line and with the ball 30 yards or so away, any shot can be judged from the framework of the goal, and will generally be dealt with in a simple, matter-of-fact way.

Recommendation: as play comes to within a distance of 35 yards from goal, the keeper retreats back to the goal line; and then recommences coming off the line to narrow the angle, or to deal with a through ball, when and only when, it seems appropriate. This will depend on the situation and the players in front of the keeper. For instance, if a keeper's own defence is goal side of the ball, there is no need to move too far off the line. A through ball, in a 1 vs 1 break-away situation, would be different.

Attacks from the Sides

If two lines were drawn from the goal line to the edge of the penalty area, as shown below, and the question was asked, "When would a goalkeeper go into the gray area?" we might get some strange answers!

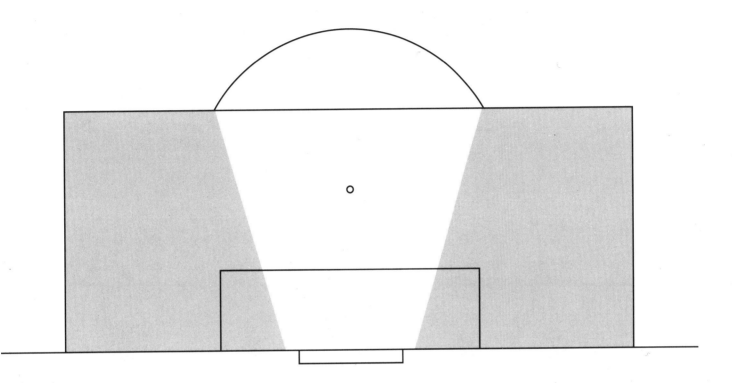

Try this one from me : "Never — unless the goalkeeper was certain of getting to the ball first." Why? If a keeper did not get to the ball first and the ball was played inside or across the goalkeeper, *the whole of the goal would then be exposed with no one else in the team allowed to use their hands.*

Young goalkeepers in particular have a habit of wandering towards the ball and away from the goal.

If the goalkeeper is to get to the ball at the side of the goal first, that's a totally different circumstance. In those type of situations the goalkeeper should "go for it"! In life, as in soccer, there are few black and white solutions. But if what I have said causes the coach to think about the sides of the goal, chances are he will be able to help the goalkeeper in these situations.

FOOTWORK

Good footwork is essential to good goalkeeping — one of the reasons for strongly promoting the "Let's Dance" sequence as a regular routine for goalkeepers.

Jumping rope is also strongly recommended. If it's good enough for world championship boxers who have to dance in-and-out of contact distances for 12 rounds, it's good enough for goalkeepers — and keepers should never get KO'd!

The "Open" KC and having the "shoulders square to the ball" ("Hands") are very important as keepers move about their goal, and particularly as they move across the goal.

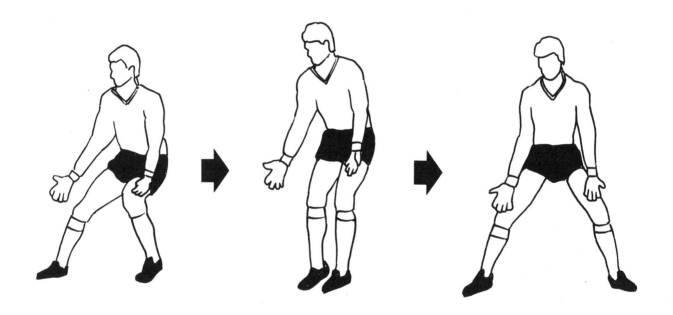

Side skipping movement across the goal maintains the "Open" position.

Normally, side skipping is the best way of moving across the goal in order to maintain the "Open" position. But when the ball is moved from one side of the goal to the other quickly, the side skips will not be effective and a faster cross-legged technique will be required. Nevertheless, while the cross-legged method is being employed the "Open to the Ball" position of the upper body can be retained.

*Moving quickly across goal with
cross-legged movement while
maintaining the shoulders square to the
ball and to the play.*

Note:

In desperate circumstances, nothing other than an all-out sprint from one post to the other is acceptable. In these circumstances keeping "open to the ball" is not worth thinking about, as the ball is already at or near the other post anyway. So getting there fast — and diving, and possibly "spreading," in a last ditch effort to prevent a goal — is the frantic, but sometimes necessary, action.

"PLAYING THE PERCENTAGES"

Because no two situations in soccer are ever exactly the same, hard and fast rules cannot be imposed on players by the coach. It is one of the great characteristics of the game. The decision-making nature of soccer puts the onus fairly and squarely on the shoulders of each and every individual player.

"Playing the percentages" is an oft-used expression amongst the Pros. What it means is that in similar situations responding in a particular way will give the highest chance of success, even though it will not work on every occasion.

It is one of the reasons we are so high on understanding the Key Considerations of Goalkeeping.

Coaches cannot do the goalkeeping, but they can place players in realistic practice situations which replicate the circumstances where a player must make good decisions — where "playing the percentages" will give a high return.

GOALKEEPER WARM-UP

Fitting the goalkeeper into the team practice, as we have outlined in this manual, does take some planning. All team practices should start with some kind of a warm-up period — including stretching activities. Goalkeepers should be encouraged to establish a stretching routine, which they can use immediately prior to practice and games.

Many warm-up activities use the ball to assist in building up the momentum.

As coach, the challenge is: Can you adjust some of your warm-ups to include a goalkeeping activity? Two examples:

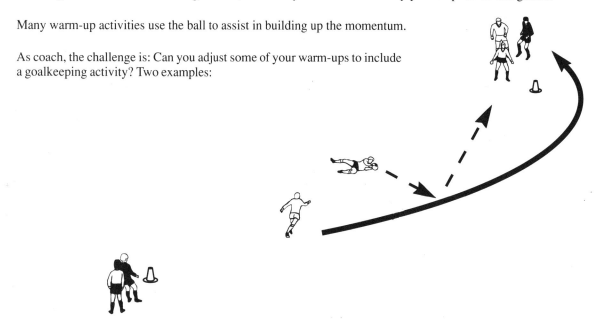

Pass/shot played to goalkeeper who rolls ball to side for shooting player to move on to and pass to the player at the front of the opposite file. Goalkeeper turns to take first time pass/shot from the next player and so on. The coach can later instruct the field players to aim the pass into the stomach of the goalkeeper. Obviously any misplaced pass will demand more of the goalkeeper — often a diving save.

Goalkeeper defends a triangular goal. Players fire a "pass" at the goalkeeper and follow the pass. The keeper fields the ball and rolls it to another player on the outside of the circle for another shot. The previous shooter continues running to take the place of the next shooter, and so on.

The keeper should attempt to change the point of the shot — and therefore the goal to be shot at each time.

PROGRAM FOR TEAM COACH

**Goalkeepers (2 or more) On Own
(or with an Assistant Coach)**

- Two Goal Practice (Page 58)

- Six-Shot Stop (Page 42)

- Wheeling and Dealing (Page 46)

- Criss-Cross (Page 48)

- Kicking (Page 47)

- Salmon Leap (Page 44)

- Let's Dance (Page 52)

- Shadow Goalkeeping (Page 54)

**Team Coach With Goalkeepers
Before/After Practice**

- Two Goal Practice (10 mins.) (Page 58)

- Six-Shot Stop (3 sets) (Page 42)

- Salmon Leap (3 sets) (Page 44)

- Diving at feet in Criss-Cross (Page 48)

- Crossing with an Attacker (adaptation of Page 72)

- Throwing/Kicking Work (Pages 46-47)

Team Goalkeeping

- Gone Fishing (Page 60)

- Through Balls (Page 62)

- Big Shot (Page 86)

- Mixed Bag (Page 78)

- Super 8's (Page 84)

- Side Kicks (Page 66)

- Near and Far (Page 72)

- Crossroads (Page 74)

BTB'S (BACK TO BASICS)

Even at the highest level of goalkeeping, some part of a goalkeeper's skill goes astray. All sports people, such as golfers and tennis players, every so often have the same problem. If a weakness surfaces there is a very good reason to go on a BTB Program for several weeks. Persistent and repetitive practice will help re-establish good habits.

WAY TO GO?

I am often asked, "What should a goalkeeper do at a penalty kick?" Or, "What did you do?" So I tell them!

I would assess the penalty kicker as he placed the ball, and take an educated guess at which way he would most likely kick it. Then I would align myself on the goal line about 6 inches off center, showing a little more of the side of the goal to which I had calculated he was going to favor — in a subtle attempt to *influence the kicker* into kicking it that way. Then, as the shooter moved to take the kick, I would fake to go to the side I had assessed he would *not put the shot* — by moving my body that way, not my feet — and then go for the corner I had predicted the shot would go.

"What would happen?"

"Usually, they would play it to the other side," I would say with a laugh.

The truth is, when I was playing in the English First Division, it was not a difficult task to keep a record of the penalty takers of each of the clubs. With a little attention to detail   — watching games, studying newspaper photographs, asking around — I was able to keep my "black book" of penalty takers, and note the way they preferred to shoot. On occasions that paid off. In a game against Liverpool FC, just after they had returned to the First Division, I "guessed" right on a penalty kick by Ron Moran. As a result, we won the game and Ron lost his penalty kicking job. Later, when I joined the coaching staff at Liverpool, and co-coached with Ron, we would joke about it.

In another game for Blackpool against Leeds United, I saved two penalties from Billy Bremner, the Scottish National Team player. We still lost 4 - 0, and Leeds had another "goal" disallowed for a disputed offside. Needless to say, I wasn't the one complaining to the referee. I've always maintained the reason I was selected for England was I saw more action in each and every game with Blackpool than any other goalkeeper in England! They say practice makes perfect! But I won't tell you about the many penalties I did not save!

SOME FINER POINTS

Collapsing One's Assets

Some of the most difficult shots for goalkeepers to save are those close to the legs of the keeper. While they may be within kicking distance, we know from the AMOB III consideration (as much of the body behind the ball as possible) that the legs and the feet alone are not reliable enough to give the percentage success rate that is acceptable.

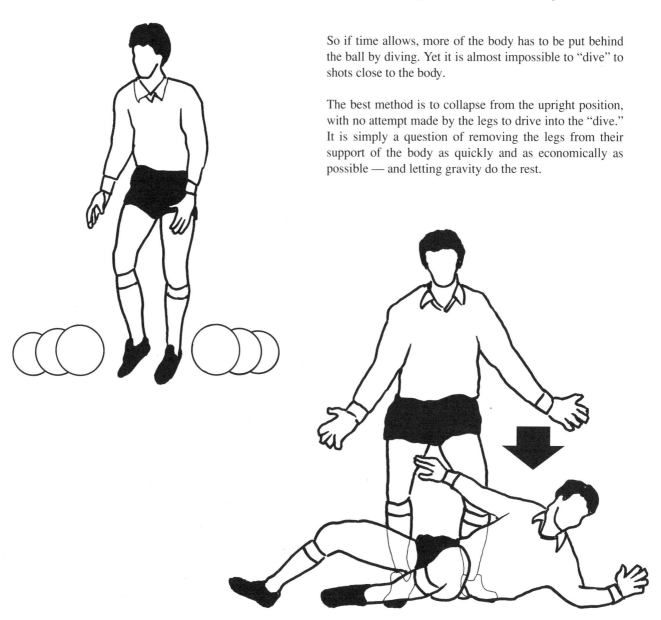

So if time allows, more of the body has to be put behind the ball by diving. Yet it is almost impossible to "dive" to shots close to the body.

The best method is to collapse from the upright position, with no attempt made by the legs to drive into the "dive." It is simply a question of removing the legs from their support of the body as quickly and as economically as possible — and letting gravity do the rest.

The "dive" is on the side — of course! It may have to be a one-handed reaction save, with the lower arm and hand extended along the ground, almost like a karate chop. If there is sufficient time, then we are back to AMOB III, with both hands leading, and all of the relevant KC's at work.

You might say that in these goalkeeping circumstances, collapsing one's assets will "save" you plenty of goals!

A Checklist of Decisions

The reason for placing goalkeepers in realistic game situations is to produce the type of learning and development that will be transferred to the "do or die" circumstances of the games themselves. Good goalkeepers don't just have good techniques. They have the ability to apply the right technique in the right situation at the right time. Also they have the knowledge to know when to do very little other than to stay "alert and alive" and let others better positioned or equipped do the job.

What follows is a checklist of decisions that would be appropriate as a Cross Ball situation is developing.

1. **Am I "alert and alive" and "ready" for action?**

2. **Is my position correct both in relation to the goal and the ball?**

3. **Are my teammates well positioned to help clear this attack?**

4. **If not, have I time to give some last second instructions?**

5. **Do I know where the most dangerous attackers are positioned?**

6. **If not, is there time to have a quick look away from the ball?**

7. **Can I give some information to the player nearest the opponent with the ball as to how he/she can affect the quality and direction of the cross?**

8. **Am I continuing to adjust my position as the play builds?**

9. **As the cross starts on its way should I go for the cross, or not?**

10. **Can I inform my teammates of my decision early?**

11. **If the decision is to come for the cross, do I need to go fast immediately, or can I delay a split second, and then come fast?**

12. **Should I punch or catch the ball?**

13. **If I have decided to stay, can I inform my players of the expected action — even delegate the responsibility to the player who should be challenging?**

The checklist could go on, and on. It is put in here to illustrate a point, which is:

There is a lot more to goalkeeping than can be covered in simple goalkeeping drills. There is the need to put keepers in testing game-type situations — particularly from 12 years of age and onwards.

Communication — The Keeper's Calling Card

I was a late developer in pro soccer. I was 22 years of age before signing my first professional player contract, which in the UK at that time made me "ancient!" Most of my teammates at Blackpool FC had been pros since they were 15 or 16 years of age.

You could argue that starting so early is not in the best interests of the all-round development of a young man, and I would agree. But that is what happened in the UK at that time, so for me it was the situation I faced.

For the first two years of my pro life I was known somewhat disparagingly as "The Amateur." It wasn't just that I had won my chance of a pro career by gaining an England amateur "cap" at age twenty one. Nor was it my attitude or application. I was far ahead of most of the "pros" in that department. It was the manner in which I conducted myself around the penalty area. At the time, I was the quietest goalkeeper in the English 1st Division.

After two years of pro soccer, I finally saw the light and started dishing out the instructions and the orders. It was only then that I finally "arrived."

Coaches must encourage goalkeepers to help their teammates by giving clear information and instructions that can be heard.

Equally important, a goalkeeper must communicate his/her intentions and decisions when moving out for a ball — particular crosses and through balls.

As well, the coach must work with the goalkeeper on the terminology and delivery of the communication. It's no good shouting "Keeper's ball!" just as the center back is in the process of heading it away. Information should be given as early as possible.

Nor is it any good whispering instructions that cannot be heard. There isn't the time in the game for a teammate to say; "Excuse me! What was that you just said?" Early, clear and loud is the way to go.

Information has to be given as precisely as possible. No time for long speeches here. But it also has to be delivered authoritatively.

I have a pet peeve about the goalkeeping utterance so common on North American soccer fields today. Goalkeepers often shout the word "Keep!" when they want the ball or are coming out for a cross. Usually it isn't one "Keep!" but a series of "Keeps." "Keep! Keep! Keep!" It sounds like a little bird chirping. The word "Keeper!" shouted with authority and sufficient decibels, sounds as if the goalie really does mean business.

PRESENCE

What makes a good goalkeeper? A list of qualities of the "perfect" goalkeeper would be a long one.

If we were to list the qualities of some of the outstanding goalkeepers of the past 20 years — Banks, Zoff, Shilton, Jennings — we would find the qualities of the individuals would not necessarily match up. Each keeper would have his own particular strengths; each would have his own weaknesses.

What all good goalkeepers do have is a "presence" in the goal and around the penalty area. It is indefinable but it is real. It's an aura built of ability, experience, authority and respect.

**To help achieve these qualities always remember the Six P's of Goalkeeping —
Practice, Patience, Persistence and Performance Produce "Presence."**

Penalties and Set Plays

The goal can be a lonely place at the best of times, but it is never more lonely than when the keeper has to face a penalty kick.

It's not quite as bad if the incident resulting in the awarding of the penalty wasn't the direct fault of the keeper. In those situations the keeper can cover himself/herself in glory, by making the save. But if it was the keeper's fault — the pressure is really on.

The penalty kick, like free kicks, corner kicks, and long throw-ins, is considered a "set play" or "dead ball" situation that directly affects the goalkeeper and requires practice and some special considerations.

As far as defending at free kicks, corner kicks and throw-ins is concerned, the goalkeeper must work out with the coach and the team the strategy and responsibilities.

At penalty kicks, there is very little the team can do other than be ready for a half-save or rebound. It's up to the goalkeeper. Practice is needed for the goalkeeper and "penalty shoot out" competitions within the practice session can be fun and beneficial.

It is not the intention of this book to go into all the detail and possibilities of set play organization nor the many possibilities of improving the chances of saving a penalty. Other than to say the chances of saving penalties will increase with practice.

Collective Goalkeeping

In spite of the protestations of this manual regarding the dangers of elitism, of isolationism, of over specialization of the goalkeeper, there remains a case for goalkeepers coming together collectively to work on the essentials of goalkeeper training.

In the practice section we have included a number of practices especially suitable for this type of collective goalkeeping situation such as the Criss-Cross, the Goalie Shootout, GK Ball, etc.

Yet no matter how much we as coaches try to integrate the goalkeeper into the team situation, chances are we will not be completely successful. Therefore, there is a case for the keeper being given "specialist" attention to enable that player the opportunity of further developing the goalkeeping skills.

This can be accomplished in several ways:

1. The team coach allocates "extra time" for goalkeeper training.

2. A club, district, state or provincial association sets aside a time for goalkeeper clinics.

3. A club or an association establishes an ongoing "Goalkeeper Academy" with weekly sessions for keepers.

4. Individuals attend specialist residential and non-residential summer goalkeeper schools.

The danger in all of this, is the keeper can once more, become "isolated" from the team. In this respect the "Goalkeeper Specialist" opportunity should be seen and used as a supplement to the team training — *and not as a replacement for team training.*

The Goal Kick

A disturbing sight on the soccer fields around the world is to see a player other than the goalkeeper taking the goal kick. If the goalkeeper has a foot injury, or a physical reason for not taking the kick, that is something else. And for young goalkeepers who cannot kick very far there is a perfectly logical reason for another player to take the kick. But at teen and adult level pulling a defender all the way back to take a goal kick is very disruptive to the defensive shape of the team and takes away some of the offside "advantage" through the team now being stretched from end to end.

Therefore, it is essential that keepers practice their kicking from the ground (goal kicks) and out of the hands. A goalkeeper who is a poor kicker is a weakness in the team, while a good kicking goalkeeper becomes a powerful team asset.

Coaches should organize and encourage goalkeepers to spend regular practice time in kicking.

Loose Fingers

How can you tell a good goalkeeper? Look at the fingers during a game or in practice. If the fingers are loose and the arms relaxed, we have a good goalkeeper!

Of course, it cannot be as simple as that. But the fingers give a very clear indication of the mode and mood of the keeper. If the fingers are extended and tense, the chances are the goalkeeper is as well.

The good goalkeeper should be relaxed (yet ready), and this will be reflected by the arms and in particular, the fingers. They should be loose, relaxed, but only the merest split second from reactive response.

Being composed, yet ready for action is essential in goalkeeping. Loose fingers can be the indicators for the coach.

200 Throws a Day

There is a small dingy gymnasium tucked away under the main stand at Blackpool Football Club. It must have been an afterthought to the original planning. But on stormy, winter days, (and Blackpool has its fair share of them) it provided a space for the Pros to have some sort of a work out.

For me it was the "Target Range." Early in my pro career it was apparent to me (not to mention most others) that my kicking was not my strong suit! But I had good throwing ability. I set out to make the "good" great!

On the end walls of this apology for a gymnasium were four ventilator grills set on each side — two near the top and two towards the bottom. They were approximately 1-foot square. The length of the gym was only 20 yards. My challenge on at least four afternoons a week, was to go into the gymnasium on my own and take 200 throws from an 18-yard mark in an attempt to hit one of the four "targets."

In my first year, I was lucky if I got 10 "hits" out of 200. After four years, I was up around 40, and my throwing had become a feature of my goalkeeping.

Moral: Persistent practice will produce results.

Goalkeeper as a Leader

We have already emphasized how important communication is in the role of the goalkeeper. The coach should encourage the goalkeeper to take a leadership role.

The goalkeeper's position at the back of the team gives a unique perspective of the game. If this is converted into information for the benefit of the other players, particularly the rear defenders, it can greatly help the team performance.

Further out from the goal, the midfielders and forwards cannot be influenced to the same extent as the back players but most of them will still be within earshot.

More often than not, around the soccer fields of the world, the team captain is a midfielder or a central defender. This is because these particular players are in the thick of things and can exert more of a "team" influence.

But a goalkeeper should be a "vice-captain" whether appointed or "unofficial."

Significantly, in the last two decades an increasing number of goalkeepers at the highest levels of the game have taken on the team captaincy (e.g. Dino Zoff, Italy; Peter Shilton, England).

At the adult level, another contributing factor that comes into play is the fact that goalkeepers usually play longer than field players. As a result they graduate to become the "elder statesmen" of the team, possessing, theoretically, wisdom and experience.

Fit to be a Goalkeeper?

Fitness for goalkeeping has not been specifically covered in this manual. But it would be wrong if we did not emphasize how important fitness is to play the goalkeeping position. For a start, it helps if the goalkeeper is not carrying excess baggage. Fitness, not fatness, is desirable because the goalkeeper position requires, at times, an athletic response to save the day.

Physical height is a factor that cannot be changed by exercise, and there is no doubt that a small goalkeeper is at a disadvantage compared to a 6-footer. Nevertheless, all goalkeepers need to work on their leaping ability and they need to strive to improve their quickness, particularly over short distances (3 to 10 yards).

Keepers have to be capable of standing up to the physical rigors and challenges that are part and parcel of life within the penalty area.

As well, agility to make saves, but also the agility to make a quick recovery is something to develop and maintain.

Most of the practices in this book will assist in goalkeeping fitness — just by repetition.

Coaches should work out a goalkeeper fitness program, which will vary from the fitness requirements of field players.

Please note: *Fitness for soccer does not become a serious consideration until players are 12 years of age and older.*

Notes